The Foreign & Second Language Educator Series

(Formerly Language and The Teacher: A Series in Applied Linguistics)

under the editorial direction of

DR. FREDERICK L. JENKS

Florida State University

The Foreign & Second Language Educator Series

Foreign-Language Testing
Theory and Practice

by

John L. D. Clark

Test Development Division
Educational Testing Service

Heinle & Heinle Enterprises
29 LEXINGTON ROAD, CONCORD,
MASSACHUSETTS 01742 U.S.A.

64066

*For Martha, James, Martyn,
and Jonathan.*

Acknowledgments

Appreciative thanks are due a number of persons who willingly contributed time, energy, and helpful observations during the preparation of this work. Mr. M. Hachemi Saada painstakingly reviewed and commented on an early draft of the manuscript, and Mr. Russell Webster made useful suggestions on material appearing in the first two chapters. Any remaining errors of fact or interpretation are solely the responsibility of the author.

Mr. Edwin York offered valuable advice on the planning of the topical index, and Mrs. Anna Jackson rendered faithful and accurate service in final manuscript typing.

A more general debt is acknowledged to the many test committee members, foreign-language teachers, and colleagues at ETS whose conversations and other professional contacts over the past several years have constituted a rich fund of information and counsel on language testing problems and possibilities.

Contents

INTRODUCTION   1
  Prognosis   2
  Evaluation of Attainment   2
    Achievement Measurement   3
    Proficiency Measurement   5
    Knowledge Measurement   6

CHAPTER 1. PROGNOSTIC TESTING   9
  General Considerations   9
  Prognosis in Foreign-Language Teaching   10
  Technical Definition of Placement   11
  The Concept of Correlation   12
  Correlation and Prognosis   13
  Selection of Criterion Measures   14
  Selection of Predictor Measures   14
    Foreign-Language Aptitude Tests   15
    Course Grades in Non-Foreign-Language Subjects   19
    Measures of Prior Foreign-Language Achievement   20
  Operation of Placement Programs   22

CHAPTER 2. ACHIEVEMENT TESTING   25
  Basic Considerations in Achievement Testing   25
    Foreign-Language Test Modalities   26
    Factors in the Selection of Test Modalities   29
      Skill to be Tested   30
      Separation of Skills   32
      Degree of Diagnostic Accuracy   34
      Use of the Native Language 38
      Ease and Reliability of Scoring   39
  Listening Comprehension   42
    Aural Discrimination   43
    Listening Vocabulary   46
    Listening Grammar   53
    General Achievement Listening Tests   58
    Response Modalities   58

Selection of Passages   60
Item-Writing Techniques   62
Item Types for General Achievement Tests   67
Interpretation of Test Scores   69
Speaking   72
  Practical Difficulties in Measuring Speaking Ability   72
  Alternatives to Formal Speaking Tests   74
    Language Laboratory Monitoring   74
    Classroom Observation   75
  Phonemic-Level Pronunciation   76
  Phonetic-Level Pronunciation   78
  Speaking Vocabulary   81
  Speaking Grammar   84
  General Achievement Speaking Tests   86
    Selection of Test Topics for "Monologue" Tests   87
    Example Topics   88
    Modalities for "Monologue" Tests   89
    Conversation-Based Tests   90
    Scoring Procedures   91
Reading   94
  Character Recognition   94
  Reading Vocabulary   96
  Reading Grammar   100
  Tests of General Reading Comprehension   103
Writing   106
  Character Formation   106
  Lexicon and Morphology   107
  General Achievement Tests   113

CHAPTER 3. PROFICIENCY TESTING   118
Linguistic Ability and Communicative Proficiency   118
Direct Testing of Communicative Proficiency   121
  The FSI Language Proficiency Interview   121
  Situational Realism of the Test Procedure   124
  Considerations in Proficiency Test Scoring   126
  Communicative Proficiency Tests for School Language
    Programs   129
Correlational Approaches to Proficiency Measurement   130

CHAPTER 4. KNOWLEDGE TESTING   133
Culture Testing   134
  Culture as Civilization and Fine Arts   134
  Culture as Patterns of Living   136
  "Explanation" of Cultural Phenomena   139

Literature Testing   140
  Reading in the Literature Course   141
  Testing of Literary Information   142
  Testing of Literary Interpretation   144

CHAPTER 5. THE ROLE OF PUBLISHED TESTS   148
  Textbook-Related Tests   149
    Textbook-Related Tests and Locally-Developed Tests   150
    Textbook-Related Tests and Standardized Tests   151
  Secure Standardized Tests   153
    General Characteristics   153
    Overview of Secure Testing Programs   154
      CEEB Achievement Tests   154
      CEEB Advanced Placement Tests 155
      Graduate Record Examinations—Advanced Tests   155
      Graduate School Foreign-Language Tests   155
      National Teacher Examinations 156
  Generally-Available Standardized Tests   156
    Overview of Recently-Developed Tests   156
    Test Development Procedures   158
    Development and Use of Norms   161
    Measurement Uses of Standardized Tests   164

REFERENCES   166

INDEX   171

Introduction

Tests in the foreign-language teaching field, as elsewhere, should not exist for their own sake but only to serve specific educational purposes. The extent to which a given test fulfills the purpose for which it is designed is the bench mark against which it must ultimately be judged. Statistical figures, norms tables, content inventories, and other technical accouterments may play a contributing role in determining the quality of a test, but the final proof must hinge on the answer to a simple and straightforward question: "How well is it doing what it is supposed to do?" Because the purpose of a test affects all of its other aspects—measurement rationale, design, use, and interpretation of results—a discussion of foreign-language testing may well begin with a description of the various measurement purposes that can be identified within the field.

It is possible to place any foreign-language testing activity into one of two broad purpose categories: *prognosis* or *evaluation of attainment*. Within each of these categories, additional sub-classifications can be made.

PROGNOSIS

It is highly desirable, both for the successful articulation of foreign-language courses and to best serve the needs of individual students, to be able to determine the most appropriate path for students to take at different decision points in their language training program. Prognostic testing attempts to fill this need by providing information on the probable future result of following a certain course of action, such as entering an accelerated language program rather than a regular one, or of specializing in a certain language field. When the decision to be made involves acceptance or non-acceptance into a particular educational program, the process is usually referred to as *selection;* when the decision involves choosing the most desirable path from among a number of alternative possibilities, the process is known as *placement.*

Measurement techniques for selection or placement vary depending on the stage in the student's language-learning career at which they are used. If the student has had little or no prior exposure to the language in question (and hence, cannot be expected to perform to any worthwhile degree on tests using that language), specially designed *language aptitude tests* must be used. These tests make use of a number of language-related exercises—such as the identification of sound-symbol correspondences and the learning of English word/nonsense word pairs—which have been found through preliminary research to predict with reasonable accuracy student success in studying foreign languages. If the student has already taken one or more courses in the foreign language, end-of-course test scores or other measures of developed competence in the language may be used for prognostic purposes. In these cases, prognosis represents a derivative or peripheral utilization of tests which were originally designed to serve other measurement functions.

EVALUATION OF ATTAINMENT

Tests in this second broad category are not intended to predict the student's future performance but rather to determine the current nature or level of his accomplishments in a particular language area. Within the evaluation-of-attainment category, three important sub-classifications can be identified, each of which involves somewhat different measurement rationales and techniques. These are: *achievement measurement* (of both diagnostic and more generally oriented types), *proficiency measurement,* and *knowledge measurement.*

ACHIEVEMENT MEASUREMENT

One of the most significant testing concerns in foreign-language courses from elementary school through the basic college level is to obtain information on the student's attainment of language skills taught in the course. This information can take the form of either highly detailed inventories showing the student's "mastery" or "lack of mastery" of a number of specific linguistic points or a more global appraisal of his achievement in broad skill areas. Tests of the highly detailed type may be labeled *diagnostic achievement tests,* and those of the broader type, *general achievement tests.*

The idea of highly diagnostic testing has generated considerable interest on the part of both teachers and test developers—an interest arising largely from the fact that of all the different types of foreign-language testing, diagnosis offers the most highly detailed information about the language accomplishments of individual students. In a day when, rightly or wrongly, depersonalization of the student is felt to be an increasing educational trend, testing procedures which are capable of giving both the teacher and the individual student a detailed profile of linguistic attainments and shortcomings are considered of utmost importance.

The primary requirement of a diagnostic test—that it indicate unambiguously the student's "mastery" or "lack of mastery" of each of the language aspects tested—places substantial limitations on the testing procedures and item types that can validly be used. Multiple-choice procedures do not for the most part lend themselves to this type of testing, not only because of the chance success factor intrinsic to multiple-choice format but also because of the impossibility, in most cases, of determining the specific linguistic aspects controlling the student's response.

Test formats in which the student actually speaks or writes a response may often be used for diagnostic testing, provided that the test item delimits the student's task in such a way that only the single desired answer would be produced by an examinee having the necessary linguistic knowledge or competence. Developing items of this type is not an easy matter, and it is necessary to be constantly on guard against the possibility that factors other than the student's competence or lack of competence in the specific language aspect tested will affect his response to the test item. For language areas in which valid diagnostic testing is possible—especially in measuring the acquisition of grammatical structures and lexicon at the early stages of instruction—this type of testing can make a substantial pedagogical contribution.

Although diagnostic achievement tests can provide useful day-by-day information on student attainment of each of many small elements of classroom work, their special nature makes them generally inappropriate as measures of the student's mastery of course content on a more global basis. Tests of *general achievement* provide for a broader view of the student's accomplishment by asking him to perform tasks more typical of "course goal" uses of the language. For example, in the listening comprehension area, rather than asking the student to discriminate spoken phonemes, to identify past, present, and future tenses in short spoken sentences, or to carry out other highly discrete tasks characteristic of diagnostic tests, a general achievement test might ask him to listen to a number of natural conversational exchanges in the foreign language and to answer questions about their content.

The measurement procedures and item format requirements for general achievement tests are somewhat less stringent than for diagnostic tests, since there is no attempt to identify the discrete elements of language skill required to answer each of the test questions. Multiple-choice format is thus frequently used, and there is less concern in preparing the test items about the specific vocabulary and grammatical structures involved in the stimulus material or the exact nature of the student's response.

There are, nonetheless, certain developmental requirements to which general achievement tests may be expected to conform. In keeping with their function of measuring the student's language *achievement* in a given program of study, test content is kept within the general framework of the student's formal course work up to that time. Some thought is also given to the representativeness of the test, that is, the degree to which the linguistic tasks which the student is asked to perform correspond both in type and proportion to those at issue during the course itself. In preparing the test, care is taken to reduce or eliminate technical shortcomings in the test questions which unfairly penalize or aid the student independently of his linguistic proficiency as such. A sufficient number of test questions are included to provide a fair and stable measure of the student's ability.

The flexibility in test development offered by the rather broad nature of a general achievement test exacts some penalty in terms of the test's informational value. Although meaningful part scores for certain sub-sections of the test can in some cases be produced, the more usual outcome of a general achievement test is a single total score which indicates only how well the student dealt with the content of the test *as a whole* and without regard to specific linguistic details of his performance. With appropriate statistical caution, students within a class can be ranked on the basis of total test score, and where normative information is available, the performance of individual students or of the class as a whole can be compared to that of larger groups of students who have taken the same test. Scores on general achievement tests can also be used for selection or placement purposes.

PROFICIENCY MEASUREMENT

Foreign-language skills courses are not taught, or at least should not be taught, for their own sake but with the intent to develop certain "real-life" language competencies in the students enrolled. "Real-life" here refers to any use of the language which takes place outside of the course setting and which has a generally accepted pragmatic value. For example, the development of a "tourist abroad" level of competence in listening and speaking would be considered a real-life goal, as would the acquisition of a "reading for enjoyment" ability by a person interested in the literature of the foreign country.

In any course of instruction aimed at developing student language proficiency for real-life purposes, the degree of student success in reaching these goals would be a matter of considerable interest both to the student—who would like to be assured that his hard work had paid off in some tangible way—and to the teacher—who would seek some confirmation that he had developed the desired proficiencies in a substantial majority of his students.

Testing procedures which are aimed at certifying the acquisition of real-life competencies may be referred to as *proficiency* tests in that they do not attempt to provide information about the student's achievement in a given course of instruction but rather to measure his ability to use the language for real-life purposes without regard to the manner in which that competence was acquired. Thus, in proficiency testing, the frame of reference—both for test development and score interpretation—shifts from the classroom to the actual situations in which the language is used. The student's performance on the test is analyzed not in terms of "how much he has learned" but in terms of how closely his performance meets the goal standards specified.

Of all the foreign-language testing techniques, proficiency testing is the least well advanced at the present time. This situation is due in part to the difficulty of defining in an objective and testable manner the linguistic aspects of typical "real-life" uses of the language, and in part to problems of administration and scoring which arise from the necessity to have the test format approximate real-life conditions. Nonetheless, because valid and usable real-life proficiency tests are so clearly needed as criterion measures of the language competencies which present-day teaching programs are intended to develop, linguistic and psychometric research aimed at the creation and utilization of tests of this type should be considered a matter of the highest priority.

KNOWLEDGE MEASUREMENT

Knowledge measurement is directed at determining the student's acquisition of facts or concepts about the foreign language or related subjects. Tests of language as a subject matter (for example, as presented in historical and comparative linguistics courses), of "civilization and culture," and of knowledge and appreciation of a foreign-language literature would all fall into this category. Although certain knowledge tests may require the student to read or write in the foreign language in responding to the test questions, the measurement emphasis is on the intellectual message conveyed rather than on the medium of expression.

Knowledge testing has acquired in the minds of many language teachers an undeservedly poor reputation—in all probability a result of the great emphasis currently placed on the development of active skills. While tests of "language as a subject matter" may indeed be unsuitable for the basic language course sequence, knowledge testing in the areas of culture and literature may be appropriate and desirable for many school programs. At the college major or graduate school level, knowledge tests assume much greater prominence, and indeed largely supplant the formal testing of language skills as such.

In the pages which follow, separate chapters will be devoted to discussions of each of the major areas of foreign-language testing which have been briefly outlined above. A final chapter describes the basic characteristics of published foreign-language tests, especially standardized skills tests, and discusses the role which these tests can play in the overall language evaluation program. The chapters are intended to be read sequentially, and presuppose the reader's familiarity with material presented in earlier sections.

A major purpose which underlies all of the discussions is that of engaging the teacher or other test user to analyze carefully and evaluate critically the measurement instruments which he uses or intends to use in a particular evaluation context. Many persons in the foreign-language teaching field (and in other educational areas as well) take an uncritical and overly trusting approach to the testing process. Such persons tend to feel that because certain booklets, recording tapes, or other materials have been labeled "tests," they are by this token certified capable of providing straightforward and valid measurement information. The truth of the matter is that the only thing which administration of a test, *qua* test, provides is one or more scores—that is to say, certain *numbers* which have come about as a result of the testing. In order for these numbers to provide pedagogically useful information, the test which generates them must be appropriate to the measurement purpose at hand. This determination in turn involves a close appraisal of the test's measurement rationale, linguistic content, format and question types, scoring procedures, and a number of other aspects which are inextricably bound up in the "meaning" of the test scores. Teachers who lack the necessary background to identify and critically evaluate these factors are quite likely to be swayed by testing fads, salesmanship, outside advice, or other such influences into developing or using tests which are not well suited to the intended purpose. Tests adopted on these bases may well have no useful informational value or may even provide information which is frankly misleading.

Teachers who do take the time and effort to become acquainted with basic principles and procedures in foreign-language testing can expect to steer a smooth course around problems of this type and to use their own or others' tests to maximum pedagogical advantage. If the following pages help the teacher or other reader to join the second group, they will have served the intended purpose.

Chapter 1
Prognostic Testing

GENERAL CONSIDERATIONS

In the field of educational measurement, prognosis refers to a procedure in which available information about students—in the form of aptitude or achievement test scores, school grades, teacher ratings, and so forth—is used to estimate or "predict" the probable degree of success that each would encounter in various courses or course programs. On the basis of this prediction, decisions are made on the advisability of having the student follow the educational paths in question.

It is important at the outset to clarify a popular misconception about prognostic measurement techniques—the notion that they operate in an autonomous manner to assign students to particular educational treatments.

The truth of the matter is, of course, that test scores or other objective data cannot of themselves make any operational decisions whatsoever. It is, rather, the teachers, department chairmen, or other administrators of the educational program who make decisions about students; and it should be emphasized in this respect that student-affecting decisions *must* be made regardless of the amount or quality of information available to aid in this task. Every spring, some students must be accepted and some rejected for attendance at a given college; every fall, a certain number of high-school language students must be placed into a certain number of available courses. If little or no reliable information is at hand about the success that students would probably encounter in following the educational programs at issue, decisions about their participation in these programs must be made either randomly or on the basis of criteria that have little or nothing to do with their potential for benefiting from the instruction offered.

Given the necessity to make decisions about students in any event, it would appear desirable to bring to bear on these decisions any available or obtainable information that has a useful degree of prognostic value. The basic question to be asked in regard to prognostic measurement is not "Should prognostic techniques be used?" (for the answer will always be yes), but rather, "What particular prognostic techniques offer the greatest potential for making correct decisions about students in a given educational situation?".

PROGNOSIS IN FOREIGN-LANGUAGE TEACHING

In the field of foreign-language teaching, the most frequent use of prognostic techniques is in connection with the *placement* of students into appropriate language courses, rather than the outright *selection* of students for participation or non-participation in a language-learning program. Although there are a few instances in which selection is considered appropriate, as in screening applicants for graduate level foreign-language study, there is a substantial consensus among teachers, administrators, and others in the foreign-language field that any interested student at the elementary or secondary school levels should have the opportunity to study a modern foreign language, and furthermore, that this study should continue over a time span sufficient to develop a useful degree of language competence.[1]

In view of this emphasis, the discussions below will concentrate on the placement aspects of prognostic testing. However, before leaving the matter of selection, it should be pointed out that essentially the same theoretical and statistical principles hold for both placement and selection. Indeed, selection may be viewed as a special case of placement in which one of the possible "placements" is rejection. Effective selection requires the use of sophisticated and highly accurate techniques: since there is usually no way in which the inappropriate rejection of particular students can be rectified, the

---

[1] See, for example, Remer (1963) and Pillet *et al.* (1967).

original selection procedure must be made as valid and as precise as possible.

Somewhat more leeway is available in the placement process, since it is possible later to move students up or down in the course sequence when it becomes apparent that the initial placement was inappropriate. Nonetheless, a high degree of prognostic accuracy is certainly a desirable goal in course placement and should be sought as actively as possible by the teacher or other person responsible for the placement program.

TECHNICAL DEFINITION OF PLACEMENT

The term "placement" has a somewhat specialized meaning when used in connection with prognostic measurement. Teachers often speak loosely of "placing" a student into eighth grade after he has completed the seventh grade, or of "placing" a student into an intermediate language course after he has taken the beginning course. Such activities do not involve placement in the technical measurement sense because there is no element of choice involved: all students completing the seventh grade will be assigned to the eighth grade, and all students completing the beginning language course will be assigned to the intermediate course. True placement in measurement terms can take place only when *two or more qualitatively different instructional courses or sequences are available to the student* and the most appropriate path must be selected from among the alternatives offered.

Some examples may be helpful. If all students completing French A are to be enrolled in French B, there is no element of placement involved. On the other hand, if the curriculum is so organized that students completing French A will be enrolled in either "French B Regular" or "French B Advanced" depending on their level of proficiency at the end of the French A course, a genuine placement situation exists. As a further example, if students are to be assigned to one of two different sections of Spanish II, taught by teachers X and Y, placement would *not* be involved if the instructional content of each of the sections is intended to be identical. If, on the other hand, it were planned that teacher X's section would proceed less rapidly than teacher Y's section and would concentrate on remedial review of grammar, the allocation of students to the two sections would represent true placement in that it would involve assigning the students to qualitatively different forms of instruction.

Before teachers or administrators undertake to administer prognostic tests or carry out other procedures aimed at "placing" students, they should assure themselves that the curriculum in fact provides for the assignment of students to different instructional programs on the basis of the data obtained. Once a genuine placement need has been established, the problem becomes that of identifying the most effective techniques for a given school setting. In order to make such a determination, the teacher or administrator must have a clear understanding of the concept of statistical correlation and its role in prognostic measurement.

THE CONCEPT OF CORRELATION

Regardless of the individual details, all prognostic measurement activities involve the same basic operation—that of obtaining those test scores, grades, teacher records, or other types of currently available information about the student which can be expected to show a high *correlation* with an appropriate later measure of success in the course or program for which the student is being considered. Many persons tend to shy away from further involvement whenever the term "correlation" is mentioned, considering it an esoteric statistical concept. Although the mathematical formula for the "product-moment correlation coefficient" is rather complicated, the real-life correspondences which it represents are quite easy to undersand.

In discussing the meaning of "correlation," it is first necessary to define the statistical term "measure." A measure is any test or other source of data which can be expressed in numerical terms. A classroom quiz, for example, is a measure, with scores ranging from 0 to 10 (or whatever). A final course grade is also a measure in that it shows students' performance in the course either on a numerical scale or in some other manner that can readily be converted to numerical form (for example, the grades A, B, C, and D can easily be rewritten as 4, 3, 2, 1).

A test or other measure is said to "correlate" with another test or measure whenever students with high scores on the first also obtain high scores on the second, and vice versa. If students line up in virtually the same rank order on both measures, the correlation between the two measures is quite high. If, on the other hand, there is no discernible relationship between students' scores on one measure and their scores on the other measure—that is, if students standing at given points in the rank order on the first measure appear "just about anywhere" in rank order on the second measure—the correlation is very low. The magnitude of the correlation is expressed statistically by the *correlation coefficient* (symbol: r) which can vary from a low of 0, indicating the complete absence of a consistent relationship between students' scores on two measures, to a high of 1, indicating a perfectly consistent relationship between the scores.[2]

CORRELATION AND PROGNOSIS

The prognostic value of a correlational relationship between two measures can immediately be seen. Whenever two measures are found to be highly correlated, it becomes possible to determine with considerable accuracy a student's probable score on the second measure simply by examining his score on the first measure. For example, if a high correlation is found between students' scores on a "predictor" test administered at the beginning of the school term and their performance on a later ("criterion") measure of accomplishment such as final course grades, then it is possible to "predict" that students who obtain a high score on the predictor test will do well in the course, and that those who do not obtain a high score on the predictor test will do less well in the course.

In the above example, the verb "predict" is used in quotation marks to indicate that no true prediction is involved here, since in order to establish the existence of a high correlation between the predictor test scores and the final course grades, it was necessary to wait until the course had ended and then calculate the correspondence between the two measures.

Use of predictor measure scores to make predictions on an operational basis would ideally take place only after one or more "dry runs" (called validity studies) had established that a usefully high correlation exists between the predictor and criterion measures *as used in the local school situation.* Unfortunately, the carrying out of such studies is more the exception than the rule, and in the majority of cases, predictor measures are chosen not on the basis of local

---

[2] *Negative* correlations, which range between zero and minus 1, can be obtained when *high* scores on one measure consistently correspond to *low* scores on the other measure. Such correlations are infrequent in prognostic measurement but can arise when the scoring scale for one (but not both) of the measures is such that better performance is represented by lower scores and poorer performance by higher scores. Negative correlations have the same predictive value as positive correlations and can be used in the same way in prognostic measurement.

validity studies but on the strength of correlations reported in other situations in which formal validity studies have been conducted.

SELECTION OF CRITERION MEASURES

Before the language department chairman or other person charged with making placement decisions begins the search for appropriate predictor measures, he would be well advised to devote close attention to the criterion measure itself. Since the criterion measure operationally defines the achievement that is to be predicted, it is of utmost importance that it accurately reflect the instructional goals of the course. For example, if the desired course outcomes include the development of listening comprehension and speaking proficiency, it would be important for the final course examination (or other measure intended to serve as the criterion) to include test sections which measure student competence in each of these areas.

If a detailed analysis of the prospective criterion measure is not made, and if final course grades or scores on some readily available test are adopted for this purpose simply "because they are there," there is a strong possibility that the prognostic procedures developed will provide little valid information about future student success in meeting course goals, even though these procedures may predict scores on the criterion measure with a high degree of accuracy. This possibility can be minimized by carefully confirming—before any prognostic measures are sought—that a student who performs well on the criterion measure can fairly be said to have attained the desired instructional outcomes of the course.

SELECTION OF PREDICTOR MEASURES

It is now appropriate to examine various *predictor measures* available for placing foreign-language students at different course and grade levels. Two broad types of placement activities can be identified: placement of *beginning students*—that is, students who have not previously studied the language in question or had any other significant contact with it—and placement of *continuing students* who have previously taken one or more courses in the foreign language.

To place continuing students, various measures of prior achievement in the foreign language can be used, as will be discussed later in the chapter. In placing beginning language students, such prior achievement measures cannot be employed; instead, it is necessary to use various measures which reflect competencies involved in foreign-language learning but which do not hinge on prior language study. Both specially designed foreign-language aptitude tests and other more general aptitude or achievement measures (such as IQ scores or grade averages in non-language subjects) can be used to place beginning language students. Of these, administration of special aptitude tests may be considered the more straightforward and more effective technique.

FOREIGN-LANGUAGE APTITUDE TESTS

Up until the mid-1950's, there were available no tests or other instruments specifically designed to predict the degree of success which a beginning language student would encounter in foreign-language courses of the "audiolingual" or "new key" type. Some "language aptitude tests" were available which served as reasonably good predictors of student accomplishment in the typical grammar-translation courses prevalent at the time, but these tests consisted for the most part of questions based on cognitive or intellectual tasks which had little relationship to—or predictive value for—the competencies called for in acquiring an active command of the language.[3]

During the years 1953-1958, Carroll conducted an extensive test development project in which he administered a large number of "language-related" test tasks to approximately five thousand students in high school, college, and military or other governmental foreign-language courses (Carroll, 1962). Those tasks which proved to have consistently high correlations with later course success and which met other statistical and technical requirements were selected for inclusion in a series of tests known as the Psi-Lambda battery and made available in commercially published form as the *Modern Language Aptitude Test* (Carroll and Sapon, 1959).

Although knowledge of foreign languages as such is not required of the student taking the *MLAT*, a number of competencies considered important to successful second-language acquisition are tested in five separate sections: Number Learning, Phonetic Script, Spelling Clues, Words in Sentences, and Paired Associates.

In the Number Learning section, the student is taught by means of a tape recording the spoken Kurdish equivalents for the numbers 1 through 4 and their "tens" and "hundreds" forms (i.e., 10, 20, 30,

---

[3] An example is the *Foreign Language Aptitude Test* (*Revised*), Iowa Placement Examinations, G. D. Stoddard *et al.*, Bureau of Educational Research and Service, State University of Iowa, 1941.

40; 100, 200, 300, 400). At the end of the learning period, the student hears several spoken number combinations in Kurdish (such as 412, 132) and indicates the appropriate Arabic equivalent in each case. In the Phonetic Script section, also administered by the tape recording, the student learns a phonetic notation system for several English phonemes and then selects the appropriate printed notation for spoken nonsense words using these phonemes. The Spelling Clues section requires the student to decipher the meaning of phonetically spelled words. In the Words in Sentences section, the student reads English sentences in which one word is capitalized and chooses among several underlined words in a second sentence the one which has the same grammatical function as the capitalized word. The final section of the test—Paired Associates—requires the student to memorize the printed Kurdish-English equivalents for 24 word pairs and then recollect these equivalents in a multiple-choice situation.

The *MLAT* requires about 60-70 minutes for administration. A "short form" of the test, which omits the first two tape recorded sections, can be given in about 30 minutes.

Correlations between the *MLAT* scores of beginning language students and various criterion measures of language-learning performance such as course grades and teacher ratings have in general been quite high, especially for "intensive" language courses which concentrate on the development of a high level of listening and speaking ability within a relatively brief time span.

A simplified version of the *MLAT* has recently been developed for use with students at the elementary school level. The *EMLAT* (*Modern Language Aptitude Test—Elementary*) (Carroll and Sapon, 1967) is administered by means of a tape recorder (all test directions are included on the tape) and requires about one hour of testing time. Although the *EMLAT* has not been so extensively standardized as the *MLAT*, administration to several hundred elementary school students in different grade groups from 3rd through 6th grades has produced correlations with final course grades or teacher ratings which are generally above .45 and in some cases considerably higher.

Pimsleur has developed a *Language Aptitude Battery* (Pimsleur, 1966) intended for use in grades 7 through 12. The *LAB* contains six parts, of which four are actual test exercises: vocabulary knowledge in English; "language analysis" (in which the student selects the correct "Kabardian" equivalents of simple English sentences on the basis of models provided); discrimination of designated sounds in spoken Ewe sentences of increasing complexity; and a sound-symbol association task in which the student hears a spoken nonsense word and marks the correct printed representation of the word.

Two parts of the battery are not test exercises but, rather, ask the student to give a self-report of his most recent grades in four non-language courses (English, social studies, mathematics, science), and to indicate, on a five-point scale ranging from "rather uninterested" to "strongly interested," his overall level of interest in studying a modern foreign language. In both of these parts, it is possible for the student to "cheat" by listing higher grades than he received or by indicating a greater personal interest in language study than is in fact the case. Student overestimation of interest in language study would have a fairly small effect on test results, since the "interest" section accounts for less than 10 percent of the total score. Incorrect listing of course grades could be minimized by asking the students to be as accurate and as candid as possible in filling out this information and by checking student responses against school records wherever possible.

Except for the "course grades" and "interest" sections, all parts of the *LAB* are administered by a tape recording. Total working time for the test is about 50-60 minutes.

On the basis of available information, it is difficult to compare the relative efficiency of the Pimsleur *LAB* and the *MLAT* in predicting foreign-language accomplishment. Both the *LAB* and the *MLAT* manuals report roughly similar magnitudes of correlation between the aptitude test and various measures of student achievement, principally course grades or scores on published achievement tests. Although these data may suggest a rough equivalence in predictive accuracy for the two instruments, it is difficult to make a firm statement to this effect in view of the varying conditions under which the two tests have been administered, that is, in different school systems using various curricula and instructional methods, and with different groups of students. In order to provide more definitive information on the relative predictive usefulness of these two tests, it would be necessary to carry out large-scale, carefully controlled studies in which the *LAB* (with and without the "course grades" and "interest" sections) and the *MLAT* (in both long and short forms) would be administered to the *same students* in each of several different courses or programs. In view of the obvious usefulness of a study of this kind, it may be hoped that the necessary experimentation will be carried out in the near future, either by test developers or by interested test users.

Formal coverage of the *EMLAT*, *LAB*, and *MLAT* in terms of the grade levels for which the test manuals state the tests to be appropriate is shown in Table 1.

TABLE 1.   RANGE OF APPLICABILITY OF *EMLAT, LAB,* AND *MLAT**

	Elementary (3-6)	Jr. High School (7-8)	High School (9-12)	College	Adult
EMLAT	√				
LAB		√	√		
MLAT			√	√	√

* As indicated in test manual.

It should be noted that neither the *EMLAT* nor the *MLAT* is claimed to be usable at the junior high-school level, and that the *LAB* is not described as applicable to college or adult populations. Experimental administration of the *EMLAT* and *MLAT* to junior high-school students would indicate whether either or both of these tests could be used validly in these grades, and trial administrations of the *LAB* to beginning language students at the college and adult levels might extend the range of applicability of this test.

There has been some interest in the possibility of using score data from language aptitude tests to make *differential predictions* about language-learning performance, that is, to determine on the basis of a student's score profile for the various sub-sections of the test whether he is likely to do well or poorly in specific aspects of the course work. Current research in this area is inconclusive. Pimsleur (1966) described his informal use of *LAB* sub-scores to predict the language-learning strengths and weaknesses of four students entering beginning French or Spanish courses. For example, one student who obtained a very low score on the "Sound-Symbol" section of the test was predicted to encounter difficulty in learning tasks involving auditory ability; this opinion was confirmed by the final course examination in which the student received a grade of "B" in written exercises but a failing grade for oral work.

Although clinical studies of this type may be suggestive of a certain degree of diagnostic value for various parts of the *LAB*, more extensive and more closely controlled investigations would be required to establish this with confidence. It is important also to note the observation by Carroll and Sapon that their studies of beginning students enrolled in Army Language School courses revealed "no reliable tendencies" for the *MLAT* or its sub-sections to correlate differentially with the students' oral or written work (1959, p. 22).

Even assuming that certain language aptitude test sub-scores were found to provide a reasonably high level of differential prediction in typical school situations, it may be wondered whether many schools would be in a position to take advantage of this information for purposes of course placement or remedial instruction. Unless the language program were set up in such a way that students with a particular learning problem (or a particular facility) for some aspect of language work would in fact receive specialized instruction, this type of diagnostic information would be of little practical value.

Experimental comparisons of the predictive accuracy of current foreign-language aptitude tests to that of various measures of general scholastic aptitude or intelligence have for the most part favored the former (Carroll and Sapon, 1959; Carroll, 1962; Pimsleur, Sundland, and McIntyre, 1964). This is not surprising in view of the fact that general scholastic aptitude tests include sections measuring a wide variety of student characteristics—such as the ability to make logical deductions, knowledge of spatial relationships, mathematical ability, and so forth—which have little bearing on foreign-language learning as such. The increased predictive power of the foreign-language aptitude tests is attributable to the deliberate selection of test tasks shown to correlate most highly with success in foreign-language learning rather than with academic achievement in general.[4]

Course Grades in Non-Foreign-Language Subjects

Course grades or grade-point averages in non-foreign-language subjects have been used with some success to predict foreign-language course grades of beginning students. Von Wittich (1962) obtained a correlation of .73 between grade-point average and foreign-language course grades of 230 beginning high school students. These results are colored somewhat, however, by the inclusion of data from a large number of students of Latin, a definitely non-audiolingual course. Pimsleur, Sundland, and McIntyre (1964) found that grade-point average and a preliminary version of the *LAB* were of equal precision in predicting final course grades in first-year high school French and Spanish courses.

It should be noted that in both of these studies student course grades were used as the criterion measure. It is not known whether similarly high correlations would be shown between grade-point

---

[4] Additional information on the theory and procedures used in developing language aptitude tests may be found in Carroll (1962). Lutz (1967) has surveyed other available literature in this area.

average (as a predictor) and a criterion measure consisting of a standardized language proficiency test or other more straightforward measure of linguistic ability. It may be assumed, however, that grade-point averages and similar indices of general school achievement would tend to correlate less highly as predictors with "pure" criterion measures of language competence than they would with course grades, which in themselves generally reflect a number of non-linguistic aspects of the student's course performance such as interest, punctuality in completing assignments, and the like.

MEASURES OF PRIOR FOREIGN-LANGUAGE ACHIEVEMENT

For students who have already taken one or more foreign-language courses, potential predictor measures include not only all those discussed for beginning students but also various measures of *prior achievement* in the language. The predictive accuracy of these prior achievement measures will depend in large part on the extent to which they reflect the student's acquisition of knowledges and skills prerequisite to a high degree of success in the course in question.

Student scores on achievement tests administered in earlier courses may be excellent predictors of performance in later courses, provided that there is a high degree of articulation between courses. Consider, for example, a first- and second-level course sequence based on a single textbook program with carefully coordinated materials. Vocabulary used in the second-level text includes and expands upon first-level vocabulary; elements of grammar introduced at the second level are based on previously taught concepts. In this situation, a year-end achievement test covering the content of the first-level course would in all likelihood be an excellent predictor of success in the second-level course, since it would reflect the student's attainment of preliminary knowledge and skills on which the second course is largely based.

On the other hand, whenever there is a sharp break in the sequence of instruction, as, for example, when different textbook programs are used or when course goals change appreciably, there is a good possibility that tests based on the content of a previous course will not measure competencies directly associated with student success in the course under consideration, and that as a result their prognostic value will be considerably reduced.

Course grades (or average grades) in previous foreign-language courses offer some potential for the placement of continuing students. The prognostic accuracy of these grades or averages will depend on the extent to which they reflect the student's actual linguistic accomplishments rather than the regularity of his attendance or other peripheral factors.[5] It is important to bear in mind, however, that grades which meet this standard are usually predominantly based on test scores or other direct measures of student accomplishment in the foreign language: this being the case, it may prove more desirable to use the test scores themselves as predictor measures rather than the "one-step-removed" course grades.[6]

A somewhat different prognostic situation is faced when continuing students from several different academic backgrounds and instructional sequences must be placed into a suitable course: a typical example is the placement of first-year college students who report one or more years of language study at the high-school level. In general, it is not possible to use grades in previous courses or other summary information provided by the sending school because of disparities in previous course content, grading standards, and so forth among the different schools. A more effective procedure would be to administer to all incoming students who report prior study of the language a locally-constructed test intended for placement purposes and providing a common yardstick against which the relative proficiency of each student can be determined. The content of the test should reflect the knowledges or skills considered prerequisite for successful work at the level for which placement information is sought. For example, if the need is to determine whether given students should be placed immediately into a second-level course or should be required to take the basic course, questions in the placement test should be concentrated on the types of achievement which the student would need to have as background for the second-level course.

If there is a close continuity between the first- and second-level courses, "alternate form" versions of classroom achievement tests actually used at the end of the first-level course would be ideal, provided that they measured general language skills rather than items of information particular to the textbook or other teaching materials used in the course. Since incoming students may not have worked with these specific materials, items which require prior familiarity with the textbook characters, knowledge of the content details of dialogues, and so forth would not be appropriate.

---

[5] This is of course on the assumption that the criterion measure itself is a relatively pure measure of linguistic proficiency.

[6] In addition, a technical benefit in using test scores rather than grades is that the former usually have a wider range of possible values and thus permit finer discriminations among students (up to the limit of test reliability).

The development of local tests for placement purposes is a laud-
able but time-consuming undertaking, and in many cases it will be
necessary to make use of a published test instead. Available instruments include: the *MLA-Cooperative Foreign Language Tests* in
French, German, Italian, Russian, and Spanish versions; the *Pimsleur
Modern Foreign Language Proficiency Tests* in French, German,
and Spanish; and a number of recent editions of the College Board
language Achievement tests which are made available to colleges
and universities under the *College Placement Test* program. The
College Placement Tests include listening comprehension and reading
tests in French, German, Italian, Russian, and Spanish. The MLA-
Cooperative and Pimsleur tests include separate tests of each of the
four language skills.

There are numerous other published foreign-language tests which
the teacher or administrator may wish to examine for placement use.
Extensive test listings appear in the *Mental Measurements Yearbook*
(*MMY*) series (Buros, ed., 1965 and earlier) and the recently published *Bibliographie Analytique de tests de langue* (Savard, 1969).

Effective use of a published test for placement purposes would
require a close prior analysis of test content along the lines suggested
for locally-developed tests. Various test reviews appearing in *MMY*
or other sources[7] might also be consulted, but this should not be considered an effective substitute for a detailed examination of the test
materials themselves.

There would seem to be little justification for administering a
foreign-language aptitude test to place continuing students, in view
of the various measures of actual foreign-language achievement available or obtainable at that time. By the same token, IQ scores or other
measures of general aptitude or of overall scholastic achievement
would appear to be of peripheral prognostic utility in comparison to
direct language achievement information available for students who
have already taken one or more courses in the foreign language.

OPERATION OF PLACEMENT PROGRAMS

The implementation of a foreign-language placement program in a
given school setting would ideally begin with a formal validity study
extending over at least one academic year. During this period, statistical correlations would be made between each of several predictor

---

[7] Clark (1965) (*MLA-Cooperative Tests*); Hakstian *et. al.* (1969)
(Pimsleur tests).

measures and an appropriate criterion measure. This activity would have two important outcomes. First, it would make it possible to compare the predictive power of each of the predictor measures used and to determine which single measure[8] could be most effectively used in later operational placement activities. Second, information provided by a formal validity study could be used to draw up an *expectancy table* which shows—within certain tolerances which arise from statistical considerations—the probabilities that students obtaining a given score on the predictor measure will obtain each of various possible scores on the criterion measure.[9] On the basis of this information, a "cutoff point" can be set in such a way that only those students expected to have a reasonably good chance of success in the course will be placed into it. For example, the results of a validity study might indicate that students scoring below 124 on a particular placement test (predictor measure) would have only a 50 percent chance of obtaining a "C" as a final course grade (criterion measure). If this is considered by the teacher or administrator to be the maximum possible "risk" level for admitting students to the course, 124 would be set as the cutoff point on the placement test. Students scoring 124 or higher would be enrolled in the course in question, while students scoring below this point would be required to take a lower-level course since they would not be considered likely to attain a satisfactory level of accomplishment in the more advanced course.

It is unfortunately the case that as a result of numerous administrative constraints and other factors, detailed validity studies are not usually carried out in connection with student placement in foreign-language courses.[10] In the absence of such studies, it is not possible either to determine on a statistical basis the relative merits of several potential predictor measures or to set specific cutoff points in terms of predicted levels of achievement.

To offset the effects of the first shortcoming, the person responsible for the placement program would have to make a close logical analy-

---

[8] In certain rather sophisticated prognostic measurement areas (such as the selection of college or graduate school applicants), data from more than one predictor measure are often combined into a composite score which is then used for decision-making. In most foreign-language course placement applications, such multiple measures would probably not be involved.

[9] Examples of expectancy tables and discussions of their use may be found in the test manuals for the *LAB* and *MLAT*.

[10] Interesting exceptions are the high school placement studies carried out by Hascall (1961) and Cloos (1971).

sis of each of several prospective predictor measures (along the lines previously discussed) to determine the one which could be expected to provide the most accurate prognostic information. The placement experiences of other school systems may provide useful leads, but this type of information cannot take the place of a close appraisal of various measures in the specific context of the local program.

In the absence of validity study data, cutoff points must also be determined on an *a priori* basis. This can be accomplished by listing students in order of decreasing score on the predictor measure and setting cutoff points to correspond to pronounced breaks in the score distribution, the maximum number of students that can be enrolled in the various courses, and so forth. This type of sectioning is necessarily somewhat arbitrary, but it is reassuring to note that, by comparison to random allocation, any cutoff system based on a ranking of students according to predictor measure scores represents an increase in the proportion of students who will be appropriately placed, assuming, of course, that there is a positive correlation between predictor and criterion measures.

Regardless of the placement techniques used, there is always the possibility that certain students will be mis-placed, either through statistical variations inherent in the placement process or as a result of changes in student motivation for language study or other individual factors. Thus, wherever possible, a trial period should be established at the beginning of the course during which students who prove to have been placed inaccurately can be moved without inconvenience or penalty into a more appropriate course or course section. A trial period of this sort also provides an informal check on the accuracy of the original placement procedure; the number of students requiring reassignment will be inversely proportional to the adequacy of the initial placement.

Chapter 2
Achievement Testing

BASIC CONSIDERATIONS
IN ACHIEVEMENT TESTING

As described in the Introduction, foreign-language *achievement testing* refers to any skills testing activities which are based on the instructional content of a particular language course and are intended to measure student acquisition of that content. This definition covers a wide spectrum of measurement concerns and testing techniques. In the beginning stages of instruction, the bulk of classroom activity usually involves the presentation and practice of small linguistic units in rather artificial settings. Examples include: the aural discrimination of speech sounds in a single-syllable or single-word context; the repetitive practice of a particular aspect of morphology or syntax; the reading of short, vocabulary-controlled sentences; and so forth. Achievement tests at this level are necessarily and desirably of a detailed, highly structured type whose primary measurement purpose is to determine whether or not the student has learned specific discriminations, grammatical patterns, or other discrete instructional aspects of the course.

In later stages of the instructional program, classroom activities acquire more and more the attributes of "real-life" uses of the language. Listening comprehension opportunities are provided not in the form of individual sounds or short phrases but in the more natural context of face-to-face conversations with the teacher on a variety of topics. Rather than working through pattern practice drills on various grammatical structures, the student begins to make active use of these structures by producing novel sentences of his own in genuine communicative situations. To reflect these changes in instructional emphasis, the nature of achievement testing itself changes. Relatively little attention is now paid to determining the student's acquisition of discrete linguistic points; instead, the tests make use of more general types of linguistic material—longer spoken passages, unglossed reading texts, stories to be related aloud by the student— which are more closely representative of the terminal language achievements sought by the course.

Achievement tests of the first type may be conveniently referred to as *diagnostic achievement tests* to indicate that they are aimed at determining student acquisition of each of a number of specific elements of course content. Tests of the second type may be described as *general achievement tests* in keeping with their function of measuring the student's ability to perform appropriately in broader areas of language use. These two basic types of achievement tests differ considerably in measurement rationale, content and format, and manner of interpretation of test results, and a discussion of the differences underlying these two types of testing, in terms of each of the four skills, will constitute the major portion of this chapter. However, it is first desirable to examine a number of theoretical and practical considerations involved in the measurement of foreign-language achievement generally.

FOREIGN-LANGUAGE TEST MODALITIES

More so than in any other school subject matter area, the validity of a foreign-language achievement test is dependent upon the format of the test questions, including especially the *modalities* in which the test questions are expressed and the student's responses given. For example, a listening comprehension test—if it is to be considered a true measure of the student's acquisition of this skill—must present spoken materials in the foreign language. By the same token, a test of speaking proficiency must be designed to elicit student speech in the foreign language. Because the question of test modalities is of such crucial importance to foreign-language testing, it is necessary for test developers and users to be clearly aware of possible modalities for various types of language tests and the advantages and drawbacks which each offers for the measurement of a given language skill or a particular aspect of that skill.

All testing activities, of whatever type, subject matter, or degree of sophistication, incorporate two major components: a *stimulus* on the part of the tester or his surrogates—the test booklet, tape recorder, or other materials or devices—and a *response* on the part of the student tested. The term *stimulus* refers to any spoken, written (including printed) or otherwise presented materials to which the student attends in the test situation and which represent or convey the testing task at issue. The term *response* refers to any physical activity on the part of the student in reaction to the stimulus materials. For example, in a multiple-choice reading comprehension test, the stimulus would consist of printed materials in the foreign language and the response would involve the marking of an answer sheet or the circling of answer alternatives in the test booklet. In a test of speaking ability, the stimulus might be in the form of a picture which the student is asked to describe aloud; the response would consist of student speech in the foreign language.

Stimuli typically used in foreign-language testing include the following modalities:
1) speech in the foreign language
2) written (including printed) materials in the foreign language
3) speech in the native language
4) written materials in the native language
5) pictorial materials (including photographs, line drawings, sets of drawings, and so forth).

Student response modalities are of two basic types: "free"—in which the student makes a spoken or written response—and "multiple-choice"—in which he simply selects an answer from among two or more alternatives. "Free" response modalities include:[1]
1) speech in the foreign language
2) writing in the foreign language

---

[1] Valette (1967) has suggested a "pictorial" response modality for listening comprehension testing in which elementary school students would be asked to draw pictures in response to spoken directions. "Action" responses—such as having the student stand up, open a window, and so forth—have been used by Asher (1969) for listening comprehension instruction and testing at various school levels. Although these two types of responses are of some usefulness for specialized testing applications, they are of limited scope in comparison to the other response modalities listed.

3) speech in the native language
4) writing in the native language.

Four sub-categories of "multiple-choice" response may be identified:

1) FL reading
2) NL reading
3) pictorial
4) pure.

When the student must read printed answer options in order to make
his response, the modality may be described as multiple-choice "FL
reading" or multiple-choice "NL reading," depending on whether the
options are in the foreign language or the native language. A "pictorial" multiple-choice modality is involved if the student must look
at a series of pictures or drawings which themselves constitute the
answer options. A "pure" multiple-choice response is one in which
there are no printed or pictured options. For example, in a listening
comprehension test, the student may be asked to determine which
of three sounds differs from the other two; his response is simply
that of marking "A," "B," or "C" on the basis of the spoken material.

Regardless of the particular sub-category, the distinguishing characteristic of the multiple-choice response in comparison to the free
response modalities is that it does not require speech or writing on
the part of the student but only the indication of a choice among
two or more alternatives. In subsequent discussions, the term "multiple choice" will be considered to include all four sub-types unless
otherwise indicated.

Of the modalities listed, spoken native language is the least useful
for foreign-language testing purposes in ordinary school settings.
Tests of simultaneous oral translation into or from the foreign
language necessarily involve spoken native language as stimulus or
response modalities, respectively, but this type of testing is at issue
only in specialized professional contexts. For regular scholastic testing
applications in which use of the native language *per se* might be
appropriate, a *written* native-language stimulus or response would
be highly preferable from a test administration standpoint.

For example, in a test of aural comprehension of spoken vocabulary items, the student might be asked to listen to a foreign-language
stimulus word and then give a native-language equivalent. Unless the
test were individually administered (as in a "live" classroom quiz),
a spoken native-language response would have to be tape recorded
for later evaluation—a much more complicated process than having
the student write the intended answer. By the same token, a written-

native-language stimulus would be much more easily administered than a spoken one and would have the additional advantage of being constantly available to the student as he makes his response.

In view of the above considerations, "spoken native language" will not be considered further as a stimulus or response modality for testing purposes. From the remaining modalities, a total of 16 different stimulus-response combinations can be obtained (Table 2).

Among the combinations shown in the table, it is necessary to rule out for foreign-language testing purposes the four shaded combinations, all of which involve stimulus-response pairs which contain no foreign-language element. From the remaining 12 stimulus-response combinations, it is possible to derive testing formats and item types suitable for all major types of foreign-language evaluation.[2]

TABLE 2.   MAJOR STIMULUS-RESPONSE MODALITIES
FOR FOREIGN-LANGUAGE TESTING

STIMULUS

RESPONSE	Spoken FL	Written FL	Written NL	Pictorial
Spoken FL				
Written FL				
Written NL			///	///
Multiple-Choice			///	///

FACTORS IN THE SELECTION OF TEST MODALITIES

Obviously, not all of the stimulus-response combinations shown are equally applicable or useful for a given testing task; indeed, the interaction of a number of factors implicit in the nature of the task reduces the feasible stimulus-response combinations to a small num-

---

[2] Carroll (1968) has developed a somewhat different taxonomy of stimulus-response modalities which the reader may wish to consult for additional background. The present classification has been drawn up independently of Carroll's formulation and differs from it primarily in the treatment of multiple-choice items.

ber of possibilities in most cases. The five most far-reaching factors
are the following:

1) the particular skill to be tested
2) the need to separate the skills for testing purposes
3) the degree of diagnostic accuracy required
4) the permissibility of the use of the native language
5) the ease and reliability of scoring.

Each of these factors will be discussed in detail in the following
pages as a preliminary to the description of formats and item types
for particular testing purposes.

SKILL TO BE TESTED

It can be considered a virtual requirement that the language skill
to be measured must figure as one of the test modalities, that is to
say: a test of listening comprehension must present spoken stimuli in
the foreign language, a test of speaking proficiency must elicit spoken
student responses in the foreign language, a test of reading comprehension must present written stimuli in the foreign language, and
a test of writing ability must arrange for the student to produce
written responses in the foreign language.

There is generally little difficulty from a technical point of view in
meeting these modality requirements for listening comprehension
and reading tests. Printed texts can easily be made available in a test
situation, and spoken materials are readily and routinely presented
by means of phonograph records or tape recordings.

Substantially greater complications are posed by speaking and
writing tests, since it is necessary for the teacher or other trained
rater to evaluate the student's spoken or written responses. In an attempt to bypass this problem, some attempts have been made to
develop multiple-choice "speaking" and "writing" tests which do not
require an active response on the student's part and which can be
graded clerically or mechanically.

Lado (1961) describes a passive test of speaking ability in which
the student pronounces a series of printed words to himself and then
selects—on a multiple-choice basis—those which are similarly pronounced. For example, given these printed options

A) UNDERST--D (past tense of understand)
B) W--D (fuel to build fires)
C) F--D (what we eat)

the student would be asked to identify the word which differs in
pronunciation from the other two (or alternatively, to designate the
two which are pronounced alike).

Use of this technique as a measure of speaking ability is based on the assumption that a covert, "recognitional" knowledge of the proper spoken response can be taken to indicate that the student can actively produce the response in a phonemically acceptable manner. Although this assumption may in general be a reasonable one, there is always the possibility that a given student will perform well on certain items of this type but make mistakes when asked to pronounce the same sounds aloud.

A second serious drawback of the passive technique is that it may be expected to have little value in motivating the student towards active speaking practice. Valette (1967) emphasizes the commonly observed fact that language students tend to concentrate on those aspects of the course which they know will be tested and cites increased student motivation for learning to speak the foreign language as one of the major reasons for the frequent administration of active tests of speaking ability.

Multiple-choice reading items considered to measure indirectly some aspects of the student's writing proficiency have been used in College Board French Achievement tests. The following style is typical:

(Select the appropriate completion.)

Aussitôt qu'elle _____ ici, préviens-moi; je veux _____ parler.

           1   2

1) (A) est   2) (A) le
    (B) sera   (B) la
    (C) soit   (C) se
    (D) était   (D) lui

Test items of this type can be considered to reflect active control of written grammar on the assumption that a student who is able to recognize correct forms would be able to produce them in an active writing situation. Even if such an assumption were to hold, the possibility of correctly answering a number of items by chance would impair the use of this and similar item types for diagnostic testing purposes, and in any event the test would have little motivational value for student writing practice.

In view of the various conceptual and practical difficulties involved in "passive" tests of speaking and writing ability, it will be assumed that actual student speech and writing are the modalities of choice for evaluating these two skills.

By applying the skill-to-be-tested constraints to the stimulus-response modalities shown in Table 2, a list of permissible stimulus-response combinations for testing each of the four skills can be derived (Table 3). Within each skill area, a number of additional factors (e.g., purpose of the testing, administration and scoring possibilities, available testing time) are involved in the final modality selection for a particular testing application.

TABLE 3.   Stimulus-Response Modalities for Testing Specific Skills°

LISTENING COMPREHENSION

Stimulus: Spoken FL

Response: Spoken FL
Written FL
Written NL
Multiple-Choice†

SPEAKING

Stimulus: Spoken FL
Written FL
Written NL
Pictorial

Response: Spoken FL

READING COMPREHENSION

Stimulus: Written FL

Response: Spoken FL
Written FL
Written NL
Multiple-Choice†

WRITING

Stimulus: Spoken FL
Written FL
Written NL
Pictorial

Response: Written FL

° Does not include "passive" testing of speaking and writing (see text).
† Including "FL reading," "NL reading," "pictorial," and "pure" subcategories.

SEPARATION OF SKILLS

Treatises on foreign-language testing commonly consider the measurement of each skill separately—that is, discuss techniques appropriate to the testing of listening comprehension, speaking, reading comprehension, and writing as separate areas of measurement inquiry (see, for example: Lado, 1961; Valette, 1967; Harris, 1969; Woodford, 1969). Similarly, standardized foreign-language test batteries regularly incorporate separate tests of each of the four skills (*MLA-Cooperative Tests, MLA Proficiency Tests for Teachers and Advanced Students, Pimsleur Modern Foreign Language Proficiency Tests*).

The notion that only one specific skill should be measured in a given test or test section may be attributed in some degree to a similar separation often drawn in foreign-language instruction. Even though language skills are usually inextricably intertwined in classroom instruction (teacher-student conversation, for example, involves both listening and speaking practice) references are still made in the teaching literature and in pedagogical discussions to a conceptual if not a practical separation of the four skills for instructional purposes.

A more significant reason for isolating a particular skill for testing purposes is the nature of the measurement process itself. Consider, for example, a multiple-choice listening comprehension test in which the student listens to tape-recorded materials and then selects a response from a number of printed options in the foreign language. Students who answer the test questions correctly may be assumed (within a margin of chance success) to have attained both a level of listening comprehension sufficient to deal successfully with the spoken materials and a degree of reading ability which permits them to understand the printed options. However, students who do not answer the questions correctly pose a considerably greater problem for interpretation, since it cannot be determined from the test results alone whether an insufficient degree of listening comprehension, an inability to read the test questions, or both, was responsible for the incorrect responses. It would of course be possible to state on the basis of the test data that the student is "insufficiently skilled in listening and/or reading," but this information would be of little pedagogical value since the implications for corrective instruction are not clear. Occasionally—and perhaps more unfortunately—the user of such a test may neglect to keep in mind the possible ambivalence of the test results and will assume that since the students are taking a test labeled "listening comprehension" the observed results can be wholly attributed to their ability or lack of ability in this skill area.

Effective separation of skills for measurement purposes does not, fortunately, require that a given test or test item incorporate only one skill element: if this were the case, test format possibilities would be seriously reduced. The requirement is, rather, that whenever two skill elements are present in a given testing situation the test user must first assure himself that students taking the test will encounter no difficulty in the second or subsidiary skill area. In the listening comprehension test example, close examination of the printed options would be required to establish that they would pose no reading difficulty for any student for whom the spoken test materials could be considered even remotely appropriate.

DEGREE OF DIAGNOSTIC ACCURACY

The requirement that a test be highly diagnostic places stringent limitations on possible response modalities. As previously mentioned, the primary purpose of diagnostic testing is to provide reliable information on student acquisition or lack of acquisition of specific linguistic elements. Thus, a basic question to be posed of any prospective diagnostic test format is whether the responses which the student is asked to make can be unambiguously interpreted to indicate proficiency or lack of proficiency in the linguistic element in question. "Free" spoken or written responses are usually straightforwardly indicative of the presence or absence of the necessary proficiency, but this is by no means so clearly the case for multiple-choice responses.

The only physical datum provided by a student's multiple-choice response is a mark on paper (or a circled letter, etc.). Of itself, a correct response to a multiple-choice question says nothing about the student's command of the linguistic feature at issue, because the way in which the response came to be cannot be determined. A devil's advocate assumption must be that the correct response was made by chance. Indeed, a person who answered a series of test items at random, and with no knowledge of the subject matter involved, would be expected to mark a certain number of questions correctly simply through the blind operation of the laws of probability. In a multiple-choice test with five answer options per item, it would be expected that 20 percent of the items would be answered correctly purely by chance. If there were only four options per item, the chance probability of correct responses would be 25 percent, or one in four.

When the testing intent is simply to obtain a general notion of the student's level of competence in a broad skill area, the chance success factor is much less critical. By including a relatively large number of items in the test, it becomes possible to discount the inflation in test scores attributable to chance success. Differential student performance in answering the remaining number of items can then be taken to indicate differing degrees of command of the subject matter of the test—when this subject matter is considered *as a whole* and without regard to the specific items that have been missed or correctly answered.

However, when the testing intent is to determine mastery or non-mastery of specific linguistic features, the problem of chance response assumes much more serious proportions since every item, in effect, becomes a miniature test. Consider, for example, a multiple-choice item in which the intent is to determine whether the student understands the meaning of the French word *chaise* when presented aurally. A suitable item type might be the following*:

[Voici une chaise.]

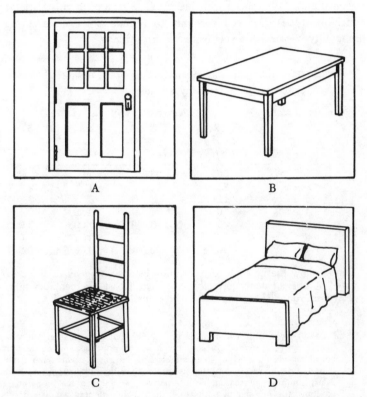

* These and other pictures appearing in this chapter, except for those on pages 55–57, 77–80, 84, and 116–117, are from *Peace Corps Language Proficiency Tests, Spoken Vocabulary.* Copyright © 1971 by Educational Testing Service. All rights reserved. Adapted and reproduced by permission.

Due to space limitations, pictures in this and following example items are reproduced in two or more rows. In operational tests, it is desirable to print all pictures for a given item in a single row.

If a student were to mark the item correctly, this would not in itself indicate that he understood the meaning of *chaise* since the correct response may have been purely fortuitous.

It is theoretically possible to reduce the chance success factor by presenting a number of "alternate form" items based on the same linguistic feature. Since the possibility of answering by chance each of a number of items decreases markedly when the number of items increases, correct student responses to each of several items testing the same point would bear out more strongly the assumption that the student had indeed acquired the linguistic competence involved.

The number of items (each based on the same linguistic point) which must be answered correctly to reduce the chance success probability to various levels is shown in Table 4.[3]

TABLE 4.   Probabilities of Answering Several Multiple-Choice
Items by Chance

Number of Items	Number of Options per Item			
	2 (A-B or "true-false")	3 (A-C)	4 (A-D)	5 (A-E)
1	50%°	33%	25%	20%
2	25	11	6	4
3	12	4	2	0.800
4	6	1	0.391	0.160
5	3	0.411	0.098	0.032
6	2	0.137	0.024	0.006
7	0.781	0.046	0.006	0.001

° Entries show the percentage probability of answering *all* of the designated number of items correctly on a chance basis. Percentages higher than 1 are rounded to the nearest whole number.

---

[3] As can be seen in Table 4, the probability that a given item (or set of items) can be answered correctly by chance also decreases when the number of answer options per item is increased. However, items having more than 4 or 5 choices are not often used in view of the difficulty of generating a large number of reasonable alternatives for a given testing point. In addition, the number of options-per-item to be adopted for a particular test or test section may be conditioned by the nature of the testing task. For example, three-choice items are appropriate for aural discrimination testing of the "ABX" type, in which the student is asked to discriminate among three sounds or short phrases the one which differs from the other two. Many grammatical structures which are inherently of a four-alternative type (such as the possible combinations of masculine-feminine, singular-plural) are most suitably tested using a 4-option format.

Unfortunately, the use of a number of items based on the same language element poses a number of practical difficulties. First is the sheer number of items that would be required to test only a few linguistic elements. If four items-per-element were considered the minimum necessary to permit a clear appraisal of mastery or non-mastery, no more than 12 different elements could be presented in a 50-item test—a highly inefficient use of testing time. Second, it would be virtually impossible to keep the items operationally independent. An alert student would be able to notice certain similarities in the items which would lead him to select the correct answers on this basis alone. In the *chaise* testing example, the fact that several panels of pictures would have a chair in common would be a very powerful clue to the correct answer in each case.

Third, the time required to score and properly interpret the test would be greatly increased by the need to add up the total number of correct responses for each language feature before determining whether the student had "mastered" that feature. The necessity to randomize throughout the test the items based on a given feature (in order to conceal the item similarities as much as possible) would make the scoring task even more arduous.

In addition to the statistical problem of chance correct response in multiple-choice testing is the more subtle but highly pervasive problem of possible linguistic ambiguity of the test item. Consider, for example, the following reading test question:

(Select the most appropriate completion of the sentence.)[4]
Es la primera vez que esta obra dramática se presenta.
Es su . . .
 (A) principio
 (B) inicial
 (C) estreno
 (D) origen

----

*(C) estreno

---

[4] The following conventions will be followed in presenting example items: General directions to the students are shown in parentheses. Entries above the dashed line denote stimulus materials; entries below the line represent the student response. The correct answer to multiple-choice items is indicated by an asterisk.

Spoken stimuli are bracketed; written (printed) stimuli are not bracketed. Spoken responses are indicated by quotation marks or phonetic transcriptions; written responses are shown in cursive handwriting.

The author of this item might assume that it is "testing" the student's knowledge of the word *estreno*. Certainly, a student who is able to read the definition provided and who also knows the meaning of *estreno* would be able to answer the question correctly. However, a student who did not happen to know *estreno* but who could rule out the other options as inappropriate would also be able to mark the correct answer. Thus, the item cannot be considered to fulfill the intended *diagnostic* function of determining whether or not the student knows the meaning of a specific word.

Except for very limited situations in which there is no or virtually no context provided along with the "tested" element (as would be the case, for example, in a simple sound discrimination item in which the student hears only isolated sounds and is asked to make a certain choice among them), it is always possible that the student will benefit from various linguistic clues provided by the item stem or the answer options in such a way as to arrive at the correct answer without definitely knowing the "tested" element.

The above criticisms of multiple-choice format are based on the assumption that the testing intent is to determine beyond any reasonable doubt that a given student possesses or does not possess a specific linguistic competence. If the test user is willing to accept a certain degree of imprecision in this respect, or wishes to evaluate the student's level of performance in more general terms, multiple-choice items can play a valid testing role.

USE OF THE NATIVE LANGUAGE

Proponents of audiolingual teaching techniques have for some years considered the use of English a *bête noire* in the foreign-language classroom, although recourse to the native language has generally been permitted to facilitate grammatical explanations and to clarify difficult vocabulary items. This tendency to avoid the use of English in instruction was quite naturally transferred to the testing area, and authorities such as Brooks (1964) urged that foreign-language tests be entirely in the target language and that English be used "only for directions" (p. 214).

Within the past three or four years there appears to have been some relaxation of the no-English dictum, at least for testing purposes. Valette (1967) has described a number of item types which use English as a test stimulus. Pimsleur (1966) described a procedure for testing various aspects of French spoken grammar by asking the student to "convey" short English sentences into the foreign language (for example, "Roger has friends" would be rendered aloud by the student as "Roger a des amis"). Educational Testing Service has recently developed multiple-choice listening comprehension tests in French and Spanish which use printed English options. These tests, intended for use in Peace Corps language-teaching programs and other programs which train listening and speaking to the virtual exclusion of reading instruction, have been administered with good measurement results and with no apparent difficulty on the part of students in alternating between spoken foreign-language and printed native-language modalities.

Jennings (1967) has cited a number of aspects of foreign-language reading comprehension which he suggests can be accurately tested only through student translation into English. These include: idiomatic expressions; special usages of prepositions, conjunctions, and other function words; and non-concrete lexicon. The testing of compound tenses in a speaking test situation is another area in which brief recourse to English (for example, asking the student to say "I will have gone" in French) would appear to provide a much more direct means of eliciting the desired response than alternative procedures which might be proposed to avoid use of the native language. (The desired tenses might be cued by marked calendars, time graphs, or other pictorial means, but the effort required to set up such conventions and to explain them adequately to the student would appear very much out of proportion to the measurement task at issue, especially when a much more direct technique is readily available.)

It would appear that the "use of English" question cannot be resolved on an across-the-board, abstract basis but only in terms of specific testing situations and purposes. A judicious orientation would be to encourage exclusive use of the foreign language for testing applications in which the desired measurement goals can be attained validly and with reasonable efficiency, but to permit the use of English whenever these criteria cannot be met using the foreign language alone.

EASE AND RELIABILITY OF SCORING

Regardless of the nature of the testing task, some means must be provided to score the student's performance—that is, to convert his speaking, writing, or marking activities into one or more numbers which correspond in some meaningful way to the quality of performance. The scoring procedure developed for any testing application must meet two important criteria. First, it must be simple and straightforward enough to be used with reasonable ease in typical school settings. Although in some instances tests which require the use of highly trained raters or complicated and expensive scoring procedures can be justified, most school uses of foreign-language tests prohibit such arrangements. Second, the scoring procedure must be *reliable,* in the sense that a given level of student performance in linguistic terms would be assigned the same or very nearly the same numerical score if the test were to be rescored on numerous occasions.

Multiple-choice format meets both of these scoring criteria in an exemplary manner. With the aid of a simple scoring key or stencil, the teacher can very quickly and easily score a multiple-choice test or, where this possibility is available, assign the task to an electronic scoring device. Scoring reliability of multiple-choice tests is virtually absolute: barring clerical errors, a given student performance (i.e., a particular answer sheet) can be evaluated again and again with precisely similar results.

Viewed strictly from the standpoint of its scoring advantages, multiple-choice format would be the response modality of preference for all types of foreign-language testing. However, as previously discussed, there are numerous situations in which multiple-choice format cannot validly be used (including the testing of writing and speaking skills and highly diagnostic testing in general) and in which a "free" spoken or written response would be required.

Some attempts have been made to evaluate spoken or written responses through mechanical means. Buiten and Lane (1965) have constructed a computer-based device capable of extracting pitch, loudness, and rhythmic parameters of a short spoken phrase and comparing these with stored criteria of correctness. Pulliam (1969) describes the development of a prototype speech interpreter, also computer-based, which can be programmed to evaluate the pronunciation of single utterances and also to recognize whether a speaker has pronounced one of several sounds, words, or short phrases previously identified as correct responses.[5]

In the writing area, a number of devices which can interpret handwritten characters are presently available, although their use in foreign-language testing has not been explicitly examined. One such device is the "optical character recognition system" (OCRS) developed by Educational Testing Service primarily for use in obtaining student names, addresses, and similar information from test answer sheets or application forms. The student carefully prints a series of

---

[5] Pulliam (1970) provides an annotated bibliography on automatic speech recognition principles and devices, with particular reference to their application in foreign-language teaching and testing.

numbers or capital letters in boxes provided, and these letters are then "read" by a computer-based device which compares the student's response to model letters stored in the computer memory.

A major drawback in the use of these and similar devices for test scoring in typical school settings is the great cost and complexity of the equipment and computer programming required. A second problem is that the scoring capability of the devices is limited to the evaluation of short, simple utterances or of writing exercises of the fill-in or short-answer type, in which each question has only one correct response or a strictly limited number of responses which can be considered correct. Tests which require longer and less carefully controlled responses on the part of the student—and which, unfortunately, pose the greatest problem for human scorers as well—cannot be scored in an effective and economical manner using mechanical evaluation devices at their present state of development. There is thus a substantial likelihood that human scorers will be required to evaluate "free response" tests for some time into the future.

The scoring reliability of a "human-scored" test can range from virtually perfect accuracy to a much less satisfactory level, depending on the training and experience of the scorer and, especially, on the inherent objectivity or subjectivity of the particular scoring task at issue. Writing or speaking test items in which the student's response is a single word or a specific short phrase can be scored with almost absolute reliability, since the scorer's task is simply that of determining whether or not the student has written in a response previously identified as "correct."[6]

The situation is somewhat more complicated when longer utterances or written passages must be evaluated for general quality. Since the student responses cannot be considered simply correct or incorrect but must be rated along a continuous scale of overall quality (or along a number of continuous sub-scales separately appraising "fluency," "appropriateness of vocabulary," and the like), some variability in the ratings assigned on different occasions or by different scorers may be considered inevitable. A Procrustean solution to the problem of scoring reliability in these cases would be to adopt some arbitrary and easily followed judging standard, such as counting the

---

[6] In a scoring reliability study for one form of the *MLA-Cooperative Writing Test* in German, a correlation of .988 was obtained between the first and second scorings (by different raters) of the single word fill-in section of the test. A section in which the student is asked to rewrite a number of sentences, changing tense, person, or other aspects of the sentence in a highly controlled manner, showed a two-rater scoring reliability of .982. (Handbook, MLA-Cooperative Foreign Language Tests, 1965, p. 24)

total number of words spoken or written. Extremely high scoring reliability could be obtained in this way, but at the expense of test validity, since under such a scoring system, the test would become a measure of the student's garrulousness rather than the linguistic quality of his speech or writing. The major desideratum in developing a scoring system for a "free response" test is to strike a suitable balance between fidelity to the linguistic attributes considered important components of response quality and the need to insure that the test can be scored with a reasonable degree of reliability.

It is unfortunate from a test development standpoint that the experimental and statistical procedures required to determine scoring reliability empirically in a given testing situation are reasonably complicated and for practical purposes impossible to implement in a classroom testing situation. Indeed, the developers of standardized foreign-language tests have themselves been somewhat remiss in this respect, and have failed to conduct large-scale, definitive investigations of the scoring reliability of their own instruments. As a consequence, scoring procedures for many types of speaking and writing test tasks must continue to be designed and used on the basis of educated guesses about the scoring reliability involved, rather than in the light of controlled experimental studies.

In the following pages, procedures will be described for testing student achievement in the four separate skill areas of listening, speaking, reading, and writing. Possibilities for the diagnostic testing of specific language elements will be discussed, as well as the development of more generally oriented achievement tests in each skill area.

LISTENING COMPREHENSION

The manner in which facility in listening comprehension is acquired by the beginning foreign-language student is not well understood at the present time. Rivers (1966) has drawn a distinction between two hypothetical levels of progress in learning to understand a spoken foreign language. The first or "recognition" level is considered to include the development of an ability to discriminate the phonemes of the target language and to perceive distinctive elements of pitch and intonation. Also included in the first level of accomplishment is the perception of structural interrelationships among the various component elements of spoken utterances. Most aspects of "spoken grammar" would be included under this rubric, including the recognition of tense cues, person, number, "actor" and "acted-upon," and other syntactically or morphologically determined features of sentence structure.

The second level of listening comprehension is considered to be that of "selection"; at this level the student has so thoroughly integrated the grammatical features of typical utterances that he is now able to pay primary attention to the semantic or "message" component of the phrases heard. According to Rivers, second-level ability cannot be effectively acquired unless the first-level perception of grammatical cues and other formal interrelationships among spoken utterances has become so thoroughly learned and so automatic that the student is able to turn most of his listening attention to "those elements which seem to him to contain the gist of the message" (p. 193).

Although the distinction made by Rivers is hypothetical and not easily verified, it does correspond rather closely to the contrast drawn earlier between diagnostic achievement testing and general achievement testing. In this regard, testing information of a highly diagnostic type would be useful during the "first stage" of instruction, in which sound discriminations, basic patterns of spoken grammar, items of functional vocabulary, and so forth were being formally taught and practiced. At this stage, the provision of information about the acquisition or lack of acquisition of specific elements of listening comprehension would be both technically possible and pedagogically desirable.

As the instructional emphasis changes from formal work on discrete aspects to more extensive and less closely controlled listening practice, the utility (and also the possibility) of diagnostic testing is reduced in favor of evaluative procedures which test primarily the student's comprehension of the "general message" rather than the apprehension of certain specific sounds or sound patterns.

This basic separation will be followed in discussing the various types of testing appropriate to achievement measurement in the listening comprehension area. Possibilities for the diagnostic testing of individual language elements will be described first, followed by a discussion of comprehension tests of a more global nature.

AURAL DISCRIMINATION

Aural discrimination tasks in foreign-language learning can be divided into two major categories: discrimination of foreign-language sounds from closely similar native-language sounds; and discrimination of foreign-language sounds among themselves, entirely within

the phonological system of the target language. In both cases, a
"pure" multiple-choice response can be considered the testing format
of preference because the focus of attention can be placed on the
spoken stimuli without any necessity for the student to read printed
options or in some other way depart from the strict aural discrimination at issue. At the most elementary level, the discrimination task
might involve determining which of three short words is different
from the other two. For example, the following item might be used
to test the discrimination of French and English /e/:

(Identify the spoken word which is *not* French.)[7]
[mes (pause) mes (pause) may]

(A)
(B)
*(C)

A similar word-triplet technique may be used to test foreign-
language/foreign-language discriminations, as in the contrast of
single R and trilled R in Spanish:

(Identify the spoken word which is different from the other
   two.)
[pero (pause) perro (pause) pero]

(A)
*(B)
(C)

Students who have learned to discriminate sounds in single-word
contexts with a high degree of accuracy may be given more difficult
tasks such as perceiving acoustic contrasts imbedded in longer
phrases or sentences:

(Identify the spoken sentence which is different from the other
   two.)

---

[7] Strictly speaking, in this item type the student is required only to isolate the "different" word among the three options. To test the student's
ability formally to label words as "native" or "foreign," a more suitable
technique would be to present a single sound which the student would
mark as "A" or "B" (or "N"-"F") for native or foreign, respectively.

[Il a tort. (pause) Il a tort. (pause) Il adore.]

   (A)
   (B)
 *(C)

In addition to using triplets of words or phrases, a number of other formats can be adopted for aural discrimination testing. For example, the student could be asked to indicate for a series of spoken words or phrases which one (or more) is the same as a previously spoken model:

(Identify the phrases which are the same as the model phrase. More than one phrase may be the same as the model.)
[Modèle: Le fou est là-bas. (long pause) Le fou est là-bas. (pause) Le feu est là-bas. (pause) Le feu est là-bas. (pause) Le fou est là-bas.]

----
 *(A)
   (B)
   (C)
 *(D)

Items of this sort offer a more difficult discrimination task than do simple triplets. However, in using them, the teacher should be careful to avoid placing too great a load on sheer auditory memory. For example, if six options were spoken for each stimulus model, even highly competent students might simply "forget" the acoustic nature of the model before they had heard all of the possible options. Further, the rules which the student must follow in making his response should not become so complex as to constitute a logical or manipulatory problem independent of the discrimination task itself. The test writer can avoid these difficulties by asking one or more persons competent in the foreign language to take the discrimination test before it is administered in the classroom. If the reviewers fail to answer virtually every item correctly, confounding factors attributable to the test format may be suspected.

Since the discrimination testing procedures described use multiple-choice format, the possibility of correct answering by chance or on the basis of peripheral linguistic information must be taken into account in determining their diagnostic validity. The fact that the items are of the "pure" type without printed or pictured options makes the possibility of correct answering through irrelevant linguistic clues unlikely, except for the possibility that the person who speaks the options will inadvertently emphasize the correct answer. The speaker should take pains to pronounce each of the stimulus words or phrases with the same intonation pattern and stress and not to emphasize the correct response in any way.

In order to reduce chance correct response to an acceptable level, it would be necessary to provide a number of items which bear on the same discrimination. Using 3-choice items, the probability that four separate items will be answered correctly by chance is about one in eighty. If a very high level of diagnostic confidence is not required, as few as two items for each contrast may be sufficient: the probability that two 3-option items will both be answered correctly by chance is one in nine.[8]

LISTENING VOCABULARY

Once the student has learned to distinguish among speech sounds in the foreign language he can begin to attach meanings to phoneme sequences representing various foreign-language words. Of the available response modalities (spoken foreign language, written foreign language, written native language, and multiple choice), written native language offers the highest degree of diagnostic precision in determining the student's acquisition of discrete elements of listening vocabulary. For example, consider the following item:

> (Write the English word which corresponds to the spoken German word.)
> [Apfel]

---

[8] These probability levels apply only to multiple-choice items which have a single "correct" answer. Chance success probabilities for items which require the student to mark more than one answer (as in the preceding example) are quite difficult to determine because of interaction effects among the answers. In using items of this type, the teacher will have to forego detailed probability information in favor of a more general appraisal of the student's discrimination performance.

If the presentation of isolated words is considered too artificial, the tested word may be used in a short sentence:

(Write the English word which corresponds to the last German word you hear.)
[Ich habe einen Apfel.]

----

apple

In both of these examples, the fact that the student must produce a free written response rather than select from multiple-choice options makes the probability of a chance correct answer extremely small: since there are a vast number of different words that could logically be supplied, the possibility of "guessing" the correct answer is highly remote. Use of this free-response technique allows the teacher to state with a very high degree of assurance that the student knows the meaning of the word *Apfel* if he writes *apple* on his test sheet and that he does not know the meaning of the word *Apfel* if he does not respond to the question or if he writes some word other than *apple*.[9]

Against the value of high diagnostic accuracy in testing listening vocabulary by means of English responses must be weighed the possibility of inculcating undesirable linguistic habits. Since there are numerous situations in which it is not possible to pair lexical items in two different languages on a strict one-to-one basis, the use of this pairing technique as a testing device—even though appropriate in this and similar instances where direct lexical equivalents exist— might have the undesirable side effect of leading the student to consider that word-for-word translation is universally possible and acceptable.

In addition to the "written native language" response modality are "spoken foreign language," "written foreign language," and "multiple choice." Spoken or written foreign-language responses would prob-

------

[9] This conclusion involves the assumption that the student is motivated to perform well on the test. If for any reason an examinee were unwilling to participate fully in the testing, or wished to conceal his proficiency, this and any other type of testing based on obtaining voluntary responses (as opposed to involuntary reactions such as pupil dilation, psychogalvanic reflex) would fail to indicate his true level of comprehension. This possibility may be safely ignored in most classroom testing, but the theoretical point is worth mentioning.

ably not be appropriate for testing listening vocabulary at basic levels since the student would not be expected to have developed sufficient proficiency in either of these "later" skills to give a definition of or otherwise identify the word in question. In advanced classes, the teacher might test certain words by asking for a spoken or written paraphrase in the foreign language, but this would probably be an infrequently used procedure in view of the fact that the student's knowledge of particular items of listening vocabulary is not usually of concern in higher-level courses.

Each of the four multiple-choice sub-types—FL reading, NL reading, pictorial, and "pure"—can be used in the testing of listening vocabulary, but with a somewhat lesser degree of diagnostic precision than is provided by written native-language responses.

"NL reading" would be involved in items such as the following:

> (Select the English word which corresponds to the last French word you hear.)
> [J'ai vu un joli chapeau.]
> (A) castle
> (B) hat
> (C) robin
> (D) picture
>
> --
> *(B) hat

This item type has no real advantage over the single-word write-in format shown in the two preceding examples, except for situations in which machine scoring is required. In addition, it fails to resolve the problem of pairing single native-language and foreign-language words.

As previously discussed, "pure" multiple-choice format does not require the student either to read printed materials or to look at printed options but simply to indicate a choice based on information presented in the stimulus itself. In terms of listening comprehension testing, this means that the answer options themselves would have to be spoken aloud, as in the following vocabulary question intended to test the student's knowledge of the French word *triste:*

> (Select the appropriate completion of the sentence.)
> [Je sais que Jean est triste parce qu'il
> (A) pleure (pause)

(B) dort (pause)
(C) chante (pause)
(D) court]

----

*(A)

This "pure" response format has the advantage of involving only the listening comprehension skill, and thus avoids the possibility that the student will encouter confounding difficulties attributable to the combining of more than one skill aspect in the test items. On the other hand, there is the disadvantage of a possible "memory load" through which the student might forget the content or sequencing of previously spoken material in the course of listening to later options.

An important technical observation should also be made at this point. Whenever multiple-choice options are themselves spoken, it is necessary to caution students taking the test not to mark their answers until all of the options have been given. If several students mark the correct answer as soon as it is heard, this will provide a clue to the other students that the correct option has just been presented. Although a no-early-marking ground rule would probably work adequately for informal classroom quizzes, there is no effective way to prevent prearranged cheating (such as might take place in a final examination) since there are many ways for students deliberately to signal that the correct response has just been spoken.

The "pictorial" multiple-choice modality offers excellent possibilities for testing those items of listening vocabulary which lend themselves to pictorial representation. Nouns describing physical objects and verbs denoting easily pictured activities can usually be tested by means of multiple-choice drawings. A number of descriptive adjectives as well as certain conjunctions and prepositions can also be effectively tested in this way. Following is an example of an item based on the auditory recognition of *marteau.*

To put the tested word in a natural linguistic environment, it may be presented in a short sentence, as shown. The sentence should provide a neutral context which gives the student no clue to the meaning of the word. A sentence such as "Pierre enfonce des clous avec un marteau" would give away the correct response to a student

(Select the object described in the spoken sentence.)
[Voici un marteau.]

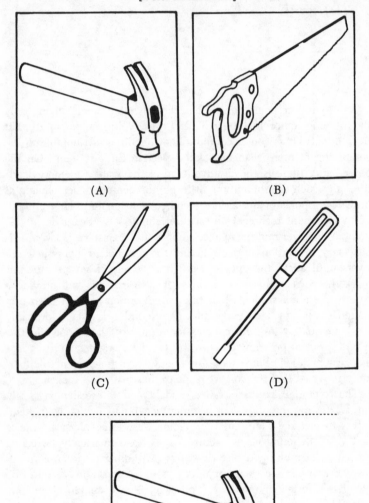

(A)   (B)

(C)   (D)

*(A)

who happened to know the meaning of *clou* but not of the ostensibly tested word, *marteau.*

Verb vocabulary can be tested through pictorial multiple-choice techniques in much the same way. For example:

(Select the picture showing the action referred to in the sentence.)

[La señora escribe.]

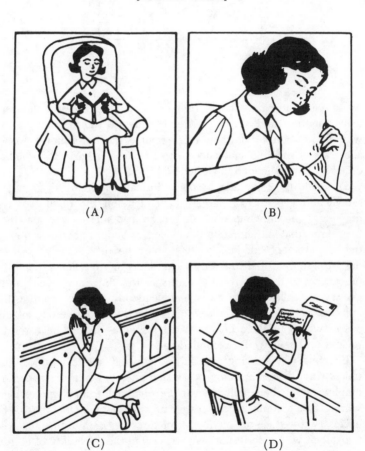

(A)   (B)

(C)   (D)

°(D)

Again, close attention should be paid to keeping the stimulus sentence "neutral" and absolutely free of clues to the meaning of the word in question. ("La señora escribe una carta," for example, would allow a student who understood *carta* to answer correctly whether or not he comprehended the tested verb.)

The validity of pictorial response formats, both in the examples shown and generally, is largely dependent on the quality of the drawings. The drawings must be prepared in such a way that they focus immediate attention on the objects or actions at issue. To meet this requirement adequately, they must be of a simple, stylized design and free of distracting background or superfluous detail. A practical way to check on the clarity of test drawings would be to ask several colleagues to guess, independently for each picture, the object or action emphasized. Pictures which are considered ambiguous or which produce unanticipated responses should be carefully revised and reviewed a second time.

Effective test drawings are surprisingly difficult to produce, and unless the teacher or some other staff member has the necessary graphic talent, help will have to be obtained from a professional source. In situations where cost is an important factor, it may be necessary to reduce the number of pictures per item to three or even two, albeit with a corresponding increase in the possibility of correct answering by chance.

The remaining multiple-choice modality is "FL reading," in which the student would read a number of printed options in the foreign

language based on the spoken stimulus.
For example:

> (Choose the definition which corresponds to the noun mentioned in the spoken sentence.)
> [J'ai acheté une cravate.]
> (A) Quelque chose qu'on mange.
> (B) Quelque chose qu'on porte.
> (C) Quelque chose qu'on boit.
> (D) Quelque chose qu'on monte.

----

*(B) Quelque chose qu'on porte.

As a diagnostically oriented test of listening vocabulary, this format has no real advantage over the pictured-option items previously discussed, except that it avoids the need to have series of pictures drawn. On the negative side, the use of written options involves a mixing of skills that may make it difficult to determine whether a given item is actually testing listening comprehension or reading proficiency. Furthermore, in writing the options, close attention must be paid to a number of important details such as keeping the sentences as short and as grammatically parallel as possible, using options which would all be equally plausible to a student who does not understand the language element tested, and so forth. For testing situations in which there is no alternative to the use of written rather than pictured options, written options can of course serve to the limit of their measurement capabilities. However, for testing listening vocabulary elements that can be clearly represented through the use of drawings, a "pictorial" multiple-choice format would be considered preferable.

LISTENING GRAMMAR

Basic to the growth of student facility in listening comprehension is the development of the ability to isolate and appropriately interpret important syntactical and morphological aspects of the spoken utterance such as tense, number, person, subject-object distinctions, declarative and imperative structures, attributions, and so forth. The student's knowledge of lexicon is not at issue here; and for that matter, a direct way of testing the aural identification of grammatical functions would be to use nonsense words incorporating the desired morphological elements or syntactic patterns. Given a spoken sentence such as "Le muglet a été candré par la friblonne," the student might be tested on his ability to determine: 1) the time aspect of the utterance (past time), 2) the "actor" and "acted upon" ("friblonne" and "muglet," respectively), and the action involved ("candré").

If such elements were being tested in the area of reading comprehension, it would be technically feasible to present printed nonsense sentences of this sort upon which the student would operate. In a listening comprehension situation, however, the difficulty of retaining in memory the various strange words involved in the stimulus sentence would pose a listening comprehension problem independent of the student's ability to interpret the grammatical cues themselves. Instead of nonsense words (which would in any event be avoided by some teachers on pedagogical grounds), genuine foreign-language vocabulary is more suitably employed to convey the grammatical elements intended for aural testing.

Many aspects of spoken grammar do not lend themselves to testing in a highly diagnostic manner because there are often only two or three possible forms for a given feature. This in turn means that chance success is a prominent factor even using free response formats. For example, the concept of number, at least in the usual classroom languages, simply involves a dichotomous classification into "singular" (one person or thing) or "plural" (more than one person or thing). A test item designed to evaluate the student's ability to identify "singular" or "plural" in response to a spoken cue necessarily represents a dichotomous choice, regardless of whether the response format is of the multiple-choice ("Circle S or P") or free-response ("Write 'singular' or 'plural'") type. To certify that a student has mastered a given singular-plural distinction—as conveyed, for example, by pronounced vs. silent final consonant in the third person present tense of regular French -*re* verbs (for example, /vã/ vs. /vãd/)—a total of four separate items on the same point would be required to reduce the chance success probability to less than one in ten.

Rather than using a number of such "alternate form" items to test a single structural element with great accuracy, test developers usually elect to forego a certain amount of diagnostic precision and to include only one item per element in a given test. Another frequent procedure—although one which results in even less diagnostic accuracy—is to pair two grammatical aspects in a single item so that four possible combinations are produced. For example:

(Select the picture which corresponds to the spoken sentence.)

[Elles vont à l'église.]

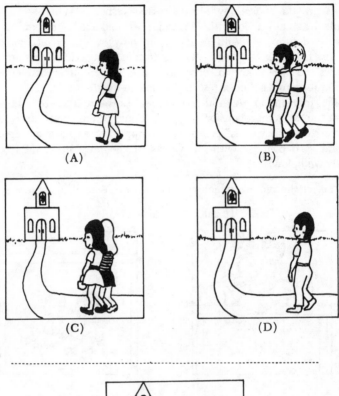

(A)   (B)

(C)   (D)

°(C)

In this item, the student is asked to make two discriminations: one between the singular and plural contrast provided by the verb form (/va/ vs. /vɔ̃/) and one between the masculine and feminine contrast provided by the subject pronoun (/il/ vs. /ɛl/). A student who grasped the "plural" aspect of the verb would presumably reduce his response choices to pictures B and C; if he were in addition aware of the "feminine" aspect of the pronoun, this would allow him to narrow the choice down to the correct response. Whether a given student actually follows this procedure in making his response cannot be determined with certainty in view of the chance success factor. However, for more general testing applications, this format allows the test maker to incorporate a greater number of elements of aural grammar into a test of reasonable length.

The four-option pictorial format can also be used to test the student's aural comprehension of prepositions, conjunctions, and other basic "function words." A Spanish example which pairs a singular-plural verb contrast with knowledge of the preposition *debajo de* is shown below:

(Select the picture which corresponds to the spoken sentence.)

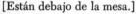

[Están debajo de la mesa.]

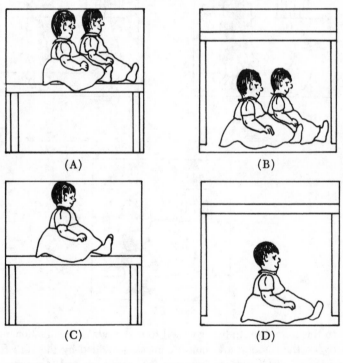

(A)   (B)

(C)   (D)

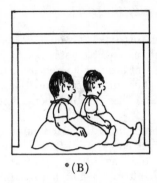

*(B)

Measurement of the student's ability to recognize spoken tense cues is not easily accomplished unless certain response conventions are adopted in a "pure" multiple-choice format or unless English is permitted as a response modality. The student's ability to pair a spoken tense with a corresponding grammatical label can be tested by according a predetermined meaning to each multiple-choice position, as shown below:

> (If the spoken sentence is in the *past indefinite* tense, mark A; if it is in the *present* tense, mark B; if it is in the *future* tense, mark C.)
> [Jean ira à l'école.]

----
*(C)

The above format has the drawback of using grammatical terminology, and teachers who do not introduce the requisite nomenclature will be unable to make use of the item type. It should also be understood that the only capacity formally tested by this format is the student's ability to associate a particular aural phenomenon with an appropriate grammatical label, not his comprehension of the "time sense" involved.

A procedure which more directly reflects the student's acquisition of the "meaning" of a spoken tense and which also eliminates the use of grammatical terminology is simply to ask the student to write the English equivalent of the tense spoken. A Spanish example:

> (Write the English equivalent of the sentence spoken.)
> [Mi amigo ha comprado un coche.]

My friend bought a car.

In writing items of this type, it would be necessary to keep the vocabulary as simple as possible so as not to present an additional confounding problem of lexical comprehension. Allowance in scoring should be made for alternate correct translations. Thus, in the present example, "bought" and "has bought" should both be considered acceptable.

Neither of the procedures discussed for testing the aural comprehension of tenses is entirely satisfactory, but the English-equivalent technique is the more straightforward and more closely diagnostic. It is difficult to see how the student's comprehension of such verb forms as "will have gone" could be tested in a diagnostic manner without asking for an English equivalent.

GENERAL ACHIEVEMENT LISTENING TESTS

The preceding examples have shown testing formats which attempt to evaluate the student's aural comprehension of certain discrete aspects of the spoken language. Tests of this type are useful to check the student's acquisition of particular elements of comprehension as they are introduced and practiced in the classroom or language laboratory, but they do not provide a wider view of the student's ability to integrate several different elements into the general performance commonly known as "getting the meaning of" a spoken passage.

Tests of *general achievement* in listening comprehension can provide total scores which reflect the student's relative degree of facility in understanding spoken passages of the type represented in the test, but by the same token they cannot be expected to indicate in any reliable or pedagogically useful way his ability to discriminate phonemes, to comprehend specific items of vocabulary, and so forth. If the measurement function of general achievement testing is clearly understood, and if the test user does not attempt to derive from tests of this type more detailed information than they are intended to provide—or can in fact provide—general achievement tests can be used in the classroom setting to give the teacher and student a useful indication of overall progress in listening comprehension.

RESPONSE MODALITIES

Multiple choice is the response modality most frequently and successfully employed for general achievement testing of listening comprehension. Of the other response modalities available in theory —spoken FL, written FL, and written NL—all can be ruled out for

one or more reasons. Spoken responses in the foreign language would
create unnecessary difficulties in administration; in addition, there is
a good chance that certain students might understand very well the
spoken passages presented but be unable to give an appropriate response due to their limited proficiency in speaking the language.

Test items based on written responses, either in English or in the
foreign language, would present fewer technical problems in administration but would pose some difficulty in scoring since the teacher
would have to decide for each of the somewhat varied written responses made by the students whether the response answered the
question properly. Some students might understand the passage but
fail to write out the key words or phrases considered "correct."
Written responses requiring use of the foreign language would also
introduce the confounding element of student writing proficiency:
since ability in handling written forms of the language is usually
developed somewhat later than is the corresponding level of listening
proficiency, the necessity to write out answers in the foreign language would make this format of questionable validity as a test of
listening comprehension *per se,* especially for students at the lower
levels.

Multiple-choice questions would obviate the administration and
scoring problems associated with spoken or written responses and
would also avoid the mixing of listening-speaking or listening-writing
skills. Of the four types of multiple-choice response—"pure," "written
FL," "written NL," and "pictorial"—the "pure" and "pictorial" formats
are probably of the least utility for general comprehension testing.
In a "pure" multiple-choice situation, both the passage and the answer options would have to be spoken, with the student merely
marking the letter corresponding to the desired answer. This technique would have the response-indication drawback previously discussed in which the students might deliberately or inadvertently
signal the correct answer immediately after it was spoken. The problem of a "memory load" would also have to be considered, especially
if the options were long or syntactically complex: in listening to
options C and D, for example, the student might fail to keep in mind
the exact content of options A and B and would thus be at a loss to
identify the correct answer. This would be even more of a problem
if the task were to select the best of several options closely similar
in meaning, because the student would have to make detailed comparisons of all of the options before arriving at his answer.

Pictorial options avoid the response-indication and "memory load"
problems but are of rather limited usefulness in testing the general
content of a spoken passage. It is difficult to design drawings which

represent the general actions or concepts at issue in whole passages, and the range of possible questions that could be asked on a given passage would be considerably restricted by the requirement that the questions be "picturable."

The two remaining formats—"multiple-choice FL reading" and "multiple-choice NL reading"—offer much greater item-writing flexibility. Printed options in the foreign language would be preferable to native-language options for use with students who can be considered to have a sufficient degree of reading comprehension ability. Options in English would of course raise the use-of-the-native-language question, but there may be no alternative for students whose training has been highly concentrated on the development of listening and speaking ability with little or no attention to reading practice. Regardless of the reading proficiency level of the students to be tested, it is highly desirable to keep any printed foreign-language options at the lowest possible level of difficulty when they are used in a test of listening comprehension.

In summary of the preceding paragraphs, the modalities of choice for general achievement measurement in the listening comprehension area are considered to be "multiple-choice FL reading" or in some instances, "multiple-choice NL reading." It should be emphasized in connection with this recommendation of multiple-choice format that the possibility of chance success—a serious problem in diagnostic testing—is of considerably less significance in general achievement measurement since the latter is concerned with appraising the student's total performance over a large number of items, rather than the exact nature of his response to individual items.

SELECTION OF PASSAGES

An initial problem in developing a general achievement test of listening comprehension is the selection of appropriate test passages. For purposes of discussion, a "passage" may be defined as one or more utterances in the foreign language—of any style or length and by one or more speakers—constituting the spoken unit on which one or more test questions are based. This definition would include such speech events as: single statements or questions by one speaker; conversational exchanges between two speakers; longer discourses by a single speaker (as in lectures, radio broadcasts, and so forth); and dramatic scenes in which two or more speakers converse at some length.

Two basic considerations are involved in selecting among possible types of passages those to be included in a given test. The first is

that the passage represent some use of the spoken language which
has a correlate in normal communication situations. All of the previously cited passage types meet this requirement: conversational utterances are a common (and usually predominant) feature of genuine
listening situations;[10] "monologues" in the form of lectures, announce-
ments, news reports, and so forth are also a frequent component of
real-life language use; and rather long dialogue sequences are involved in plays or other dramatic presentations.

There are, however, certain other types of speech which—although
occasionally included in listening comprehension tests—are not encountered in real life, except possibly in a very infrequent and exceptional way. The reading aloud of descriptive passages from a novel
would fall into this category, as would the presentation of illogical
or nonsensical utterances typically included in "true-false" tests ("The
snow is green," "Cats have six legs," etc.). Although listening comprehension of a sort is involved in these passages, they do not reflect
the types of speech that the student would encounter in the actual
listening situations toward which his training is presumably directed,
and for this reason would be considered inappropriate in tests of
general classroom achievement.

In addition to making sure that the comprehension passages used
in the test reflect real-life uses of the spoken language, the teacher
should be careful to include only those types and styles of spoken
discourse to which the students have had formal classroom exposure.
While listening *proficiency* tests can legitimately present listening
situations which reflect the types and frequencies of language use
involved in real-life "goal" behavior of a certain type (e.g., effective
travel as a tourist)—and on this basis incorporate test content that
may not have been taught in a given instructional program—it would
not be a fair measure of a student's *achievement* in the program to
ask him to listen to types of spoken materials that had not constituted
part of the work of the course. For example, if the students have not

---

10 It must be admitted that the conversational exchanges usually presented
in tape recorded listening tests are relatively formal, "purified" versions of
the frequently hesitant, redundant, and ungrammatical speech typical of
actual communicative situations. (See Abercrombie, 1963 for additional
discussion.)

　　Listening comprehension tests in French and Spanish which include
live, unplanned conversations on various topics have been developed by
Educational Testing Service for use in a Peace Corps testing project. Initial results indicate that students encounter much greater difficulty in understanding these "natural" conversations than the prepared dialogues
typical of current listening comprehension tests.

been introduced to spoken materials typical of drama, radio broadcasts, and the like, the use of these types of passages in a test of course achievement would be questionable.

Test passages may either be taken direct from "genuine" sources or prepared by the teacher. Short conversational utterances can usually be written by the teacher, but longer passages are difficult and time-consuming to prepare and in addition run the risk of being somewhat stilted and unidiomatic unless the teacher has a high degree of proficiency in the language and is also closely attuned to the niceties of style and lexicon involved in different styles of speech. Tape recordings of radio broadcasts can provide a rich source of potentially useful passages, and excerpts from dramatic scripts may also provide suitable test passages.

Regardless of the source from which the listening passages are obtained, the teacher should carefully review the lexical and grammatical content of each passage. It is not necessary or desirable to edit out of a listening comprehension passage every grammatical or syntactical element which the student would not have encountered during the instructional program. The inclusion of an occasional word or construction with which the student would probably not be familiar should be considered acceptable *provided that* knowledge of this element is not important to the general meaning of the passage or crucial to the answering of the test items. However, the overall level of difficulty should be well within the capabilities of the better students in the course, and for the most part the words and structures used in the passage should be those to which the students have previously been exposed.

ITEM-WRITING TECHNIQUES

The writing of valid and effective multiple-choice items for listening tests and other applications is a challenging task which requires both effort and acumen on the part of the teacher. Although the pointers shown below will acquaint the teacher with some of the basic considerations in multiple-choice item writing, extensive item-writing practice is necessary to master the many technical and practical details involved.

1) *The items should not be answerable on the basis of outside knowledge.*

A pervasive problem in multiple-choice testing is the possibility that the test items can be answered correctly on the basis of "outside knowledge"—general information which the student brings to the test from some other source and which permits him to answer one or more questions correctly without necessarily having comprehended the test materials on which the questions are based. For example, if a group of students were asked to listen to a news report on the most recent U.S. space flight and to answer questions about it, students who were close followers of the space program might be able to answer correctly all or most of the questions simply on the basis of their own knowledge of the area. Outside knowledge does not rule out the possibility that a particular student can also comprehend the passage presented, but it raises a real (and insoluble) doubt about the provenance of the correct answers.

Passages and questions based on scientific principles, historical accounts, subject matter of other academic areas, interviews with famous personages, well-known plays, and so forth are especially susceptible to contamination through "outside knowledge" and should be closely examined by the teacher with this possibility in mind.

> 2) *Correct responses should not hinge on a memory capacity beyond that expected of an average native speaker of the language.*

The short-term retention of the informational content of spoken utterances is incontestably one of the factors involved in listening comprehension and, indeed, the foreign-language student should be expected to demonstrate such a capacity in working with listening test materials. However, he should not be expected to retain from the stream of speech specific details which a native speaker of the language would probably not remember. Dates, street names and other locations (unless emphasized), enumerated items ("I bought some apples, peaches, a head of lettuce, and a dozen oranges"), and many other peripheral aspects of a spoken passage are largely ignored by the native speaker, who instead concentrates on the major communicative elements of the passage. In this regard, it would appear inappropriate to attempt to train—and by the same token, to test— the student's ability to bear in mind those aspects of spoken utterances which are not usually attended to by the native speaker.

In preparing test questions on a particular passage, the teacher can effectively guard against testing the student's "memory-for-details" by asking a native speaker or other person proficient in the test language to listen to (note: not read) the proposed passage and to attempt to answer each of the questions posed. If the correct answer is not immediately apparent, a memory factor may be suspected and the item should be carefully reviewed.

3) Passage length should be carefully correlated with the number of questions asked.

This caution is not appropriate for single-utterance or short-dialogue passages on which only one question is usually based, but it does apply to longer passages which are followed by two or more items. If a very long passage (on the order of two hundred words or more) is accompanied by only two or three test items, this represents an inefficient use of testing time since it is necessary for the student to listen to a large quantity of spoken material in order to answer a relatively small number of questions. If, one the other hand, an excessive number of items are written on a rather short passage (for example, five items on a passage of under one hundred words), it is likely that at least some of these items either will have overlapping content (i.e., will ask the same question in slightly different terms) or will appeal to some detail which is not a legitimate part of the main informational theme of the passage and is thus suspect for testing purposes.

It is not possible to give an overall rule for the number of items that should be developed for passages of different lengths because the many types and styles of passages vary widely in the "richness" of their content and in the ease with which they lend themselves to significant comprehension questions. A general guideline would be to ask as many questions as possible on each passage, while at the same time being careful to avoid basing questions on points that are not clearly emphasized in the passage.

It is generally more advisable to make up a test of several shorter passages, each with two or three items, than to base a similar total number of items on only one or two longer passages. This will avoid inordinately penalizing students who for some reason are not well attuned to the material presented in a particular passage and will at the same time provide a wider and more representative sampling of passage types and content.

4) The test items should conform to important technical and linguistic criteria.

In order to fulfill their measurement purpose, multiple-choice items must be carefully prepared in accordance with certain technical and language-related guidelines. First, the written options should be as short as possible while at the same time conveying the necessary information. Experienced item writers are often able to reduce the answer options to single words or short phrases, as in the following example:

(Select the most appropriate reply to the spoken question.)
[Comment vont vos amis à Paris?]
(A) Tout de suite.
(B) Oui, merci.
(C) Très bien.
(D) Deux ou trois.

----

*(C) Très bien.

Since the student has only a certain amount of time to respond to each item, the use of short options reduces the possibility that he will exhaust the allotted time attempting to read through the answer alternatives. For listening comprehension tests especially, the reading load posed by the printed options—both in terms of the number of words and their linguistic complexity—is a factor which must be kept constantly in mind by the item writer.

Second, the incorrect options should be designed to appeal to the student who has only partially understood the stimulus material or who has gained an erroneous impression of its meaning. In the example above, options A and D are intended to attract the student who mentally confuses the adverb *comment* with *quand* or *combien*, respectively.

Teachers familiar with errors commonly made by students are usually able to create plausible but incorrect "distracters" of this type. Each of the incorrect options should be carefully designed to have at least some (hopefully, strong) appeal to students who have not comprehended the stimulus material fully. On the other hand, the incorrect alternatives should not be so close in meaning to the correct answer that competent students would be in doubt as to the proper response. Any student who has thoroughly grasped the meaning of the test stimulus should be able immediately to select the correct answer after only a cursory inspection of the other alternatives.[11]

---

[11] Considerable developmental work remains to be done in the area of option-writing for foreign-language testing. Although experienced test writers are usually able to write distracters which are empirically effective (in the sense that they are chosen by students who do not have a strong command of the material tested), the procedures followed in generating these distracters have for the most part not been clearly expressed or subjected to close theoretical and experimental analysis.

The most thoroughly elaborated approach is that involving contrastive linguistic analysis and described most extensively by Lado (1961; see also 1957). On the basis of a detailed comparative analysis of the linguistic systems of the native and target languages, distracter options are prepared

Third, the options should all be equally specific or equally general. Assume, for example, that a listening comprehension passage has been presented and that the student is asked the following question:[12]

[What is the man talking about?]
(A) The weather.
(B) Clothes.
(C) His visit to the national shrine.
(D) Sports.

The fact that alternative C is so much more specifically oriented than the other three options is a clear suggestion to the student that this must be the correct answer. It is by no means necessary to restrict possible answer options to such general categories as A, B, and D in this example, but care should be taken that all options are at a similar level of generality or specificity.

Fourth, when a series of items accompany a single passage, the teacher should guard against the possibility that certain clues appearing in one item will point to the correct answer for another item.

---

so as to exemplify errors which the student would be predicted to make when he attempts to transfer linguistic habits in his native language to the target language. Upshur (1962) has pointed out that this approach, although possibly applicable for students at the beginning stages of foreign-language study, does not take into account the learning which takes place as the student progresses in his mastery of the target language and which alters the configuration of linguistic knowledge and habits which the student brings to the test.

A second criticism of the contrastive approach is that tests developed on this basis are appropriate only for students with a single specified language background, since they are "tailor made" to reflect learning problems particular to a given native language-target language combination. Although this would not be a consideration in regular school testing (where students usually have the same native language), it would be an important factor in developing tests to be administered to students from many different language backgrounds (for example, in testing the English proficiency of foreign students applying to U.S. colleges or universities).

In the absence of a more systematic approach to the item-writing problem, the classroom teacher must rely on his commonsense ideas of the types of distracters that would be effective in a particular test item. To supplement this intuitive knowledge, the teacher may wish to keep a record of errors typically made by the students in free-response situations (classroom conversations, language laboratory work, composition writing, etc.) and to use this as an additional source of potential distracters.

[12] For convenience of discussion, this and the following two items are presented in English.

For example, consider the following pair of items for which the passage is not shown:

[Who went to the beach?]
(A) Mr. Smith
(B) Mr. and Mrs. Jones
(C) The Jones' daughter
(D) Mr. Smith's friend

[What did Mr. and Mrs. Jones build in the sand?]
(A) A medieval castle
(B) A dam
(C) A walled city
(D) A fort

Students unable to answer the first question on the basis of the passage would be easily able to guess the correct answer in light of the information provided by the second item.

Although painstaking care in the original writing of test items can help the test maker to avoid these and other problems, it is highly desirable that one or more additional persons be asked to review the test before it is administered. The suggested review would be carried out in two steps. First, reviewer(s) proficient in the test language would be asked to guess the correct answer to each item without listening to or reading the stimulus material: this procedure would help to identify the various item "giveaways" discussed. Following this review—and after any necessary test changes—one or more persons competent in the language (preferably other than the original reviewers) would actually take the test; any difficulties encountered in answering particular questions, or any tendency to mark incorrect options as correct, would suggest the need for additional changes in the passages or items before the test is administered operationally.

ITEM TYPES FOR GENERAL ACHIEVEMENT TESTS

A number of different types of items can be used to test listening comprehension at the general achievement level. These can be divided into two separate categories depending on whether the items are used alone or form part of a set. The former type, often called "discrete" items, usually consist of a relatively short spoken stimulus which can be either a single utterance by one speaker or a short (two-to-four-utterance) dialogue between two people. Lengthier dialogues, or conversations among three or more people, are more profitably accompanied by a set of several items in view of the greater amount of language material represented and the consequent opportunity to pose more than one question on passage content.

The following discrete item corresponds closely to real-life conversational situations in which the student would be addressed by an interlocutor. Comprehension of the spoken stimulus is tested by asking the student to select the reply that would most logically be made to the stimulus statement or question.

> (Select the most appropriate reply to the spoken statement.)
> [La circulation dans les rues est très difficile à cause des voitures.]
> (A) Il faut avoir de la patience.
> (B) Il faut consulter un médecin.
> (C) Il faut la mener au garage.
> (D) Il faut beaucoup travailler.

> °(A) Il faut avoir de la patience.

Another type of discrete item reflects listening situations in which the student overhears a short conversation in which he does not participate. The question following the dialogue can ask about many different aspects of the situation, including the general topic of discussion, the identity of the speakers, the location of the conversation (e.g., in a grocery store, at the bank), or more specific points.

> (Listen to the conversation and answer the question about it.)
> Man: [Wie viel kostet dieses Hemd, Fräulein?]
> Woman: [Das weiss ich nicht, mein Herr. Ich bin nicht die Verkäuferin.]
> Test voice: [Wer spricht?]
> (A) Ein Gast und eine Kellnerin.
> (B) Ein Mann und seine Tochter.
> (C) Ein Ladeninhaber und eine Verkäuferin.
> (D) Zwei Kunden in einem Geschäft.

> °(D) Zwei Kunden in einem Geschäft.

The following shows a listening passage with a set of items:

[Le ministre de l'Education Nationale, accompagné de sa charmante épouse, est arrivé ce matin dans notre ville où il assistera à l'inauguration du nouveau lycée de filles. Il a été accueilli à sa descente d'avion par monsieur le maire ainsi que par un groupe d'enfants des écoles qui ont remis à la femme du ministre un beau bouquet de fleurs.]

    [Avec qui le ministre est-il venu?]

    (A) Avec le maire.

    (B) Avec ses enfants.

    (C) Avec le président.

    (D) Avec son épouse.

----

  *(D) Avec son épouse.

    [Pourquoi est-il venu?]

    (A) Pour un concours d'aviation.

    (B) Pour inaugurer un établissement scolaire.

    (C) Pour prendre des vacances.

    (D) Pour visiter une exposition de fleurs.

----

  *(B) Pour inaugurer un établissement scolaire.

An alternative procedure for both the passage/item format and the preceding "dialogue" format is to print the item questions on the student's test paper rather than (or in addition to) speaking them. A major drawback of this technique is that students familiar with this type of testing may deliberately read over the test questions before the passage is spoken and thus gain an unfair listening advantage over less "test-wise" students. This situation could be corrected by formally instructing the entire class to read the questions before the passage is spoken, but the test would then no longer parallel a "real-life" listening situation because the students would have an advance indication of important passage components. The more desirable procedure would thus appear to be to restrict the questions to aural presentation. The questions should be short and simply phrased to avoid the possibility that students who had understood the spoken passage quite well would not be able to answer one or more items correctly due to linguistic complexities in the questions themselves.

INTERPRETATION OF TEST SCORES

As emphasized previously, measurement information provided by general achievement testing procedures consists of a total test score based on the student's performance on the entire test rather than on specific items. Since different students can arrive at the same total score by answering correctly different combinations of items, the specific linguistic attainments represented by identical scores may vary considerably. It is of course possible to examine student responses to individual items, but it is inappropriate to conclude that correct or incorrect answers to these items unambiguously denote "mastery" or "non-mastery" of specific linguistic elements, both because of the chance success factor associated with multiple-choice item types and because of the general impossibility of isolating from the linguistic complexities of the test item a single element which is both necessary and sufficient for a correct answer to that item.

In interpreting the student's total score on a general achievement test, the teacher should also keep in mind that a certain number of items must be considered to have been answered by chance. This figure may be determined by dividing the total number of items in the test by the number of options per item. Thus, on a 40-item test using 4-option items, each student would be expected to answer ten items correctly on a chance basis without necessarily having comprehended any of the test materials. In analyzing results for this test, the teacher would not consider that a given student had demonstrated even a slight degree of competence unless his test score were somewhat about 10.

Test scores above the chance level can be used to compare the performance of different students provided that the teacher is careful not to interpret small differences in student scores as indicative of true differences in ability. To express the variability inherent in a test score, a statistic known as the *standard error* is used. The numerical value of this statistic depends on a number of factors, especially total test length. Calculation of the standard error of a test score for a given test requires fairly elaborate computations, and most teachers will have neither the patience nor the statistical expertise required to make these computations. Diederich (1964) has developed the following table[13] for estimating standard errors of scores when it is not possible to derive the exact values:

---

[13] Here revised slightly from the version shown in the referenced work on the basis of a personal communication from the author. The Diederich document may be obtained—together with several other pamphlets on classroom testing, selection of published achievement tests, and other measurement topics—in a *Tests and Measurements Kit* (Educational Testing Service, n.d.) available free of charge to teachers and other educational personnel.

On tests of up to 50 items, the standard error of an individual score is

0 when the score is zero or perfect
1 when the score is 1 or 2 points from zero or perfect
2 when the score is 3 to 7 points from zero or perfect

On longer tests and beyond these extreme scores, the maximum standard error of an individual score (rounded to the nearest whole number) is

3 on tests of 24-47 items
4 on tests of 48-79 items
5 on tests of 80-119 items
6 on tests of 120-167 items

To determine whether the test scores of two students are significantly different, that is, whether they can be considered to represent a true difference in performance rather than random statistical variations, the teacher must make appropriate allowance for the standard error of scores. This is done by squaring each score's standard error, adding the two squares, and taking the square root of this sum. Test scores which do not differ by at least *twice* the obtained figure[14] should not be considered indicative of a true difference in student ability.

For example, consider a 50-item test and two student scores of 28 and 42, respectively. From the table, the estimated standard error of each of these scores is found to be 4. The two standard errors are then squared ($4 \times 4 = 16$; $4 \times 4 = 16$), added ($16 + 16 = 32$), and the square root taken ($\sqrt{32} = 5.66$). Doubling this figure gives 11.32, which for convenience and additional measurement safety is rounded upward to 12.

In order to reflect true performance differences, the two test scores in question would have to differ by at least 12 points. Since the observed difference between them is 14 points, the teacher may with some confidence assume that the two students differ in achievement on the subject matter of the test. However, in comparing other scores (such as 27 and 36), the teacher may not be able to make this assumption, and should instead consider that the students in question do *not* differ in the linguistic abilities reflected in the test.

In addition to using general achievement test scores to compare student performances, the teacher may be interested in knowing

---

[14] This corresponds to a chance probability level of .05 (i.e., there would be only five chances in a hundred that score differences this large would be obtained solely through the operation of chance factors).

what information the test score gives about the student's linguistic performance. The only firm statement that can be made is that the student has reached a certain, numerically expressed, level of proficiency in dealing with language tasks of the types and degrees of difficulty represented by the test as a whole. If a listening comprehension test has presented various passages typical of radio broadcasts, stage plays, and lectures, the total score should be viewed as representing the student's level of performance on a *composite* of listening tasks of these types. If the teacher wished to have a separate indication of student proficiency in each of these three listening areas, it would be necessary for him to administer a different test for each area (i.e., a test containing only passages from that area) or, alternatively, to develop a quite long test with a separate subtest for each area. In the latter case, each subtest would have to contain a sufficient number of items to minimize the chance success factor and to provide for meaningful discriminations among students. In effect, this would amount to giving three different tests within a single test framework.

In terms of the diagnostic value provided, tests of the general achievement type must frankly take second place to the diagnostically oriented achievement tests described earlier in the chapter. On the other hand, general achievement tests are superior to their diagnostic colleagues in their ability to present longer and more realistic segments of the foreign language and thus permit a more meaningful appraisal of overall linguistic performance.

SPEAKING

PRACTICAL DIFFICULTIES IN MEASURING SPEAKING ABILITY

Evaluation of student speaking ability is the most difficult—and by the same token the most challenging—area of foreign-language skills testing. This is due in large part to the inherent nature of the spoken response and its consequences for test administration and scoring. An important consequence is the need for additional testing equipment and special administrative arrangements beyond those required for tests in other skill areas. In reading and writing tests, the only items of "equipment" needed are test booklets, pencils, and (in some cases) separate answer sheets; listening comprehension tests require in addition a phonograph or tape recorder to present the test stimuli. All of this equipment is readily available and routinely used in most school systems. Speaking tests, on the other hand (except for those which are directly administered and scored by the teacher on a "real-time" basis, such as individual face-to-face interviews), require in addition some means of recording the students' responses to the test stimuli. Language laboratories equipped for student recording at the booth positions offer the most efficient means, since a number of students may be tested simultaneously up to the maximum number of recording positions available. Schools lacking the necessary laboratory facilities must arrange to test students individually using two portable tape recorders—one to play the test tape and the other to record the student's responses. In either case, the administrative complexity substantially exceeds that involved in tests of the other three skills.

Second, spoken responses present technical difficulties in scoring as a result of the fleeting nature of the response. Listening, reading, and writing tests provide a written record of the student's answers which is constantly available and easily consulted during the scoring process. By contrast, spoken responses may be listened to only once in a face-to-face interview situation; in tests recorded for later evaluation, student responses can be re-heard only with difficulty because of the need to shuttle the tape back and forth to locate the desired material.

A third consideration is the great amount of time required to administer and score speaking tests, even in relatively low-volume applications such as the testing of a single school class. Consider, for example, a five-minute test to be administered to thirty students. In an interview testing situation, minimum administration/scoring time would be 2½ hours (running time of the interview multiplied by the number of students tested). The actual time required would probably be three hours or more in view of the inevitable scheduling delays, needed rest periods, and so forth.

Administration of a tape-recorded test would require an even longer amount of time. Under the most favorable conditions (i.e., using a language laboratory equipped to record all students simultaneously), total administration/scoring time would be no less than 3 hours 15 minutes, assuming that 15 minutes are needed to administer a test yielding 5 minutes of student recording and that only one minute per student is lost in tape mounting and rewinding during the scoring process.[15] This figure is probably an underestimate of the

---

[15] Rude (1967) suggests that language laboratory assistants can be assigned to re-record a number of student test responses onto a single reel of tape, thus reducing the time required by the teacher for tape handling. This would facilitate the teacher's scoring task somewhat but would involve additional staff time and effort in making the second recording.

time actually required, since it assumes that the teacher works at top efficiency in tape handling, makes all necessary student identification and scoring notations while the tape is running, and listens to all of the tapes without interruption or backtracking to re-listen to particular responses. Four hours would be a more typical figure, taking these additional factors into account.[16]

<h2>ALTERNATIVES TO FORMAL SPEAKING TESTS</h2>

Even teachers who enthusiastically support the development of speaking proficiency as a classroom goal may be taken somewhat aback by the amount of time required to test student attainment of this skill in a formal way. In this regard, there is a natural interest in the possibility of making at least a limited appraisal of student speaking ability in the course of regular classroom or language laboratory work. Although such approaches are admittedly "better than nothing," they have numerous drawbacks as effective measures of speaking accomplishment, especially from a diagnostic standpoint.

LANGUAGE LABORATORY MONITORING

Stack (1966) suggests that the teacher can routinely appraise students' language laboratory work on pronunciation exercises or pattern practice drills by briefly listening in to each student's booth position and evaluating whatever response he happens to be making on a three-point scale of "excellent," "neither excellent nor poor," and "poor." The limited usefulness of such a procedure for diagnostic testing is immediately apparent in that it does not provide any way of identifying the particular phonological or structural point at issue in a given response.

If the teacher is willing to forego diagnostic potential, monitoring techniques of this sort may over the course of a school term tend to identify students whose language laboratory work—of an unspecified nature, and varying with each student—was "excellent," "neither excellent nor poor," or "poor," but this is scant information even in general achievement terms. Furthermore, most persons would not consider the speech situations represented by the usual laboratory drills to be closely similar to those which the student would encounter in

---

[16] Cartier (1968) makes the suggestion that speaking test tapes could be re-recorded using a mechanical speech compression device so that the tests could be scored at an appreciably faster rate. Although such a procedure is not currently feasible for classroom testing situations, it has considerable interest from a theoretical and developmental standpoint.

the real-life contexts toward which his training is directed and which a general achievement test would attempt to reflect.

CLASSROOM OBSERVATION

Some attempts have been made to develop rating scales for the teacher to use in evaluating students' classroom speaking performance. O'Rourke (1962) presents a "Class Pronunciation Test—Scoring Scale" which the teacher is intended to fill out for each student on a daily basis. Within each of 14 rating categories (e.g., "general pronunciation," "cadence," "intonation," "phrasing," "liaison," "speed," "clarity"), the teacher rates the student's performance as "superior," "average," or "poor." Guerra, Abramson, and Newmark (1964) describe an "Oral Ability Rating Scale" to be used in evaluating oral production (including both language laboratory and classroom work) at the end of junior and senior high school courses. Pronunciation quality of the student's "echo ability," "recitation," and "drill," and the fluency, correctness, and aptness of his "drill responses" and "directed responses" are rated on five-point scales ranging from "unintelligible, inaudible, or no response" to "intelligible and with native intonation."

Reliability information is not shown for either rating scale, and it is an open question (though probably doubtful) whether the classroom teacher—on the basis of impressions gained in the course of day-to-day work with the students—would be able to rate each student's performance accurately according to the rather detailed categories shown. The clerical implications of these and similar rating scales are also worth noting. The conscientious use of daily (or even weekly) rating forms would be a formidable undertaking for any class of more than a few students, and the time and effort involved could easily exceed that required to administer and score a number of formal speaking tests, either in tape-recorded or live-interview format.

In the following discussions, it will be assumed that the teacher has decided that the measurement potential of laboratory monitoring or informal classroom observation is not sufficient for his purposes and wishes instead to develop a more explicit and more objective program for evaluating student speaking performance. Possibilities for diagnostic testing will be considered first, followed by a discussion of more general tests of speaking ability.

Measurement techniques of a diagnostic sort can be usefully applied in the areas of pronunciation, spoken vocabulary, and spoken grammar. Included in the *pronunciation* category would be tests of the student's ability to pronounce sounds or groups of sounds in a phonemically acceptable manner (i.e., in a manner comprehensible to native speakers of the language), or in a phonetically acceptable manner (i.e., in a manner indistinguishable from the pronunciation of native speakers). Tests of *speaking vocabulary* would be used to determine the student's ability to produce words from memory in response to appropriate stimuli; and tests of *speaking grammar* would measure the student's ability to produce appropriate morphological and syntactical patterns in a given speech situation without regard to vocabulary knowledge as such. Each of these three areas of diagnostic testing is discussed separately below.

PHONEMIC-LEVEL PRONUNCIATION

Student acquisition of foreign-language pronunciation at a phonemic level of accuracy is a very useful accomplishment. Once the student is able to produce each of the foreign-language sounds in a comprehensible manner, it becomes possible for him to forget about pronunciation problems in large part and to concentrate on developing grammatical control, learning new vocabulary, and increasing his overall speaking fluency.[17]

It is not necessary to teach (or by the same token, to test) those foreign-language sounds which have a phonemically acceptable "counterpart" in the student's native language. Contrastive phonological comparisons of English and the target language[18] point up in a formal way the commonsense observations of foreign-language teachers that the "English" versions of many foreign-language sounds are entirely comprehensible to native speakers of the target language and as such these sounds do not require explicit classroom instruction.

On the other hand, sounds which do *not* have a comprehensible counterpart in English are valid objects of instruction at the phonemic level, and tests must be developed to determine whether or not the student has acquired the necessary pronunciation accuracy. The author has conducted an experimental study of French speech sounds which made use of a quite rigorous procedure for testing phonemic-level pronunciation (Clark, 1967). In this study, a panel of native

---

[17] It is understood, of course, that an increasingly close approximation to phonetic standards of accuracy would be a continuing goal of most courses, even though a workable phonemic level had already been attained by the students.

[18] See, for example, Stockwell and Bowen (1965) (Spanish), Moulton (1962) (German), Agard and Di Pietro (1965) (Italian), and Politzer (1965) (French, Spanish, German).

speakers of French were asked to determine for each student-produced sound whether the sound was "comprehensible" in the sense that they could think of a French word in which that sound appears.

Although desirable from a theoretical standpoint, a testing procedure of this type could not be used in the average school setting because of the many technical complexities involved (e.g., the necessity to randomize presented sounds, to tabulate and analyze scorers' responses, etc.). For practical testing purposes, it is necessary to assume that the classroom teacher will be able to make valid and consistent judgments on the comprehensibility or lack of comprehensibility of a given student pronunciation. This assumption has not been investigated experimentally, but it appears likely that most teachers who are reasonably competent in the target language and who keep constantly in mind that comprehensibility (rather than phonetic identity with a native model) is the judging criterion should be able to assign a "pass-fail" ("comprehensible-not comprehensible") score to heard sounds with a useful degree of accuracy.

A suitable testing format would be to present pictures identifying common nouns and to ask the student to pronounce the word in question. For example, an item to test French /y/ might be as follows:

(Say what you see in the picture.)

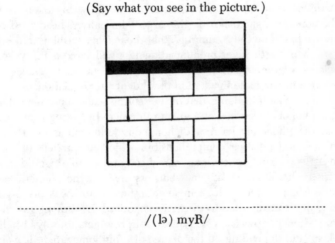

/(lə) myR/

It should be emphasized that *phonetic* details would not be at issue here: for example, the student's /y/ could be highly diphthongized and still be accepted as phonemically correct.

In addition to the pictorial format shown above, "written foreign language" and "written native language" stimuli may be used for phonemic-level pronunciation testing. Examples of these item types are shown in the following section on phonetic-level testing. The item format would be the same in both the phonemic and phonetic cases, but the scoring criteria would, of course, differ.

PHONETIC-LEVEL PRONUNCIATION

The testing of pronunciation at the level of *phonetic* accuracy would ideally be carried out using a number of native speakers to judge whether students' pronunciations of given sounds were in fact indistinguishable from native sounds when the two were mixed randomly in a judging situation.[19] Technical and administrative considerations would, however, make this procedure unfeasible for use in a regular school context, and it is again necessary to look to the teacher as the judge of pronunciation accuracy. Whereas most teachers would probably be able to judge the *phonemic* acceptability of their students' pronunciations, teachers who are not native speakers of the language or who have not had training in phonetics may not be able to make the necessary discriminations accurately at the phonetic level. However, teachers who do not consider themselves qualified to evaluate closely the phonetic aspects of student pronunciation would also probably not stress the development of phonetic-level pronunciation in their courses and by this token would not be concerned with testing this aspect formally. The discussions below are based on the assumption that the teacher wishing to design and use a phonetic-level pronunciation test will have a fairly good knowledge of the articulatory phonetics of the target language and experience in the close evaluation of student pronunciation.

An immediate question is that of the scoring scale to use in evaluating the phonetic accuracy of a given utterance. In testing pronunciation at the phonemic level, a dichotomous judgment is clearly implied: a sound is either comprehensible or not comprehensible, and an in-between category such as "partly comprehensible" would make no sense. The situation is somewhat less clear in the phonetic case because it is possible, at least in some instances, to speak of varying degrees of approximation to the native standard. Diphthongization of certain French vowels is a typical mispronunciation by English speakers, and depending on the degree of diphthongization, it would be possible to say that a response "meets the native standard" (no diphthongization), "departs somewhat from the native standard" (moderate diphthongization), or "departs considerably from the na-

---

[19] This technique is described in Clark (1967).

tive standard" (severe diphthongization), or to use some other continuous scale.

Although a continuous scoring scale might be suitable for use with
certain foreign language sounds, there are other situations in which
the student's response—at the phonetic as well as the phonemic level
—would be either "correct" or "incorrect" without any possibility of
gradation. For example, phonetically correct pronunciation of the
Spanish consonant /đ/ can be taught simply by asking the student to
pronounce an English /d/ but to change the point of articulation
from alveolar to interdental. From both articulatory and acoustic
standpoints, the change from /d/ to /đ/ is immediate and dichotomous or, to put it another way, there is no way for the student to
pronounce a sound which is "in between" /d/ and /đ/. Whenever
the nature of the speech sound to be learned is such that the student's
pronunciation of it can be considered only "correct" or "incorrect,"
a scoring scale based on finer discriminations would not correspond
to the acoustic realities of the situation.

For sounds which can at least in theory be scored in greater detail,
the question of scoring reliability for the more detailed scale may be
raised. To the author's knowledge, rigorous studies comparing the
scoring reliability of dichotomous and of 3 (or more)-point scales
have not been carried out in the foreign-language pronunciation area,
although the information provided by such studies would be of great
practical value. An impression, gained from informal contact with
various types of sound-evaluation systems, is that "right"-"wrong"
scoring—in which the listener simply rates each sound on whether it
is correctly (in the phonetic case, natively) or incorrectly (non-na-
tively) pronounced—leads to less ambiguous and considerably more
rapid marking than is possible using more detailed rating scales. For
the reasons discussed, the use of a dichotomous "native"-"non-native"
scoring system in testing phonetic-level pronunciation would be considered the most suitable procedure.

A common technique to elicit student utterances in phonetic-level
pronunciation testing is to present short spoken phrases in the foreign
language which the student is asked to imitate as closely as possible.
The major objection to this technique is that it represents a sound
mimicry situation rather than a sound production situation: students
who are able to pronounce a given sound accurately immediately
after hearing it spoken might not be able to produce it with similar
accuracy in the un-cued situations typical of most real-life speech.

If the use of spoken foreign-language models in a sound-imitation
format is not considered an appropriate procedure, "written foreign

language," "written native language," and "pictorial" modalities may be proposed. Of the three, written foreign language would probably be the least desirable since it would raise the possibility of orthographical influences. For example, if the student were asked to read a printed sentence such as "Es un lobo" (to check the phonetically accurate pronunciation of the Spanish /ƀ/), he might be led to pronounce an occlusive /b/ under the influence of the printed letter, even though he would normally pronounce /ƀ/ in a pure speech situation.

A pictorially-based item testing the phonetic-level pronunciation of French /R/ is shown below:

(Name aloud the object you see in the picture.)

/(la) Rɔb/

In using pictorial format—for both phonemic-level and phonetic-level testing—the teacher should be careful to insure that the pictured words will be familiar to the students taking the test and that the pictures will not elicit any words other than those intended. If in the preceding example the student were to say nothing in response to the picture or were to say *jupe,* this would tell the teacher something about the student's spoken vocabulary level or the clarity of the test picture, but would provide no information about his ability to pronounce /R/.

"Written native language" could be used as a stimulus modality for pronunciation testing by presenting English words whose foreign-language equivalents would incorporate the sounds to be tested. For example:

(Say aloud the Spanish sentence which corresponds to the English sentence.)

I see the moon.

/beo la luna (yo beo la luna)/

An advantage of this format over the preceding pictorial technique is that whole phrases can be elicited, making it possible to test pronunciation aspects such as obligatory liaison and vowel and consonant modification across word boundaries.[20] A potential disadvantage, in addition to the use of English *per se,* is that an atypical or incorrect translation may fail to contain the sound in question. This possibility can be minimized by using the simplest possible words and structures in the stimulus phrases.

It should be emphasized that the student's ability to give a phonetically accurate pronunciation of a foreign-language sound in a specific phonetic environment does not necessarily imply that he can produce the sound with similar accuracy when it appears in a different environment. For example, if a student were found to pronounce French /R/ acceptably in the test word *robe,* this does not warrant the assumption that his pronunciation of this sound would be equally accurate in the word *gras,* in view of the considerably greater articulatory difficulties posed by the inclusion of the /R/ in this and other consonant clusters.

On the other hand, it could be assumed on the basis of the *robe* results that the student would also be able to pronounce /R/ acceptably in phonetically similar contexts such as *ride, rade, rame, robinet,* and so forth. Teachers of foreign-language phonetics can usually identify sound production situations which are similar and dissimilar from an articulatory point of view and would be in a good position both to specify the desired content for a diagnostic pronunciation test and to assist in the interpretation of results.

SPEAKING VOCABULARY

As previously defined, *speaking vocabulary* refers to the oral production of foreign-language words in response to an appropriate stimulus. Pictorial cues are perhaps the most desirable type of stimulus for eliciting spoken vocabulary since they do not bring into play any other foreign-language skill besides speech and do not require

---

[20] "Written foreign language" stimuli would also be suitable for this purpose.

use of English. The chief disadvantage of pictorial stimuli for vocabulary testing is that the words tested can only be those which are easily and straightforwardly "picturable." These are for the most part limited to concrete nouns and to verbs denoting actions. For example:

(Name aloud the object shown in the picture.)

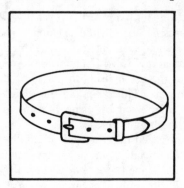

"(der) Gürtel"

(Look at the picture and name the action taking place.)

"La mujer plancha."

The student may be instructed simply to give the infinitive form of the verb or to give a short sentence describing the action taking place.

In the latter case, only the verb would be considered in scoring.

Vocabulary items which cannot readily be elicited by means of pictures can in some cases be tested using another stimulus modality. Spoken or written native language can be used to establish a context in which only a given foreign-language word would be appropriate. The stimulus may be either a single word in the native language which the student translates orally into the foreign language or a phrase or sentence in the native language which describes or defines the intended foreign-language word. For example:

(Say the foreign-language word corresponding to the English word.)

Tuesday

"martes"

brother

"hermano"

(Say the foreign-language word suggested by the context.)

A person who delivers mail is a . . . . . .

"cartero"

If the use of English is not permitted, the above item type could be used with a spoken or written foreign-language stimulus:

L'homme qui distribue des cartes postales et des lettres s'appelle un . . . . . .

"facteur"

If a foreign-language stimulus is used, the teacher should check carefully that the vocabulary and phraseology of the stimulus would present no comprehension problem. In the above example, "des cartes postales et des lettres" has for this reason been used in place of the more precise term *courrier*.

In testing spoken vocabulary, the teacher should not be concerned with accuracy of pronunciation beyond the phonemic level, since the measurement intent is simply to determine whether the student has certain words available to him to use comprehensibly in speaking situations.

Speaking Grammar

The testing of speaking grammar is an interesting and challenging undertaking for the test designer, and since the ability to form spoken sentences in a morphologically and syntactically accurate manner is one of the basic components of speaking proficiency, diagnostic information on specific student attainments and shortcomings in this area can be of considerable pedagogical value.

Pictorial stimuli are in general not well suited to the testing of speaking grammar because it is extremely difficult to design a picture or series of pictures which will elicit specific structures and no others. For example, consider a situation in which an attempt would be made to test use of the reflexive construction in French. A picture such as the following might be used:

The anticipated response to this picture would be a phrase containing the verb *se laver,* such as "Elle se lave," "La jeune fille se lave," or "Elle (La jeune fille) se lave les mains." Students who gave one or another of these sentences could be considered able to produce reflexive constructions acceptably, at least in contexts similar to those represented by the test item. If, however, the student were to reply "Elle (La jeune fille) fait sa toilette," this would be a perfectly acceptable response to the picture but would not provide any information on the student's ability to use reflexive constructions. In a face-to-face testing situation, the teacher could of course ask the student if there were "some other way" in which the picture might be described, but this possibility would not be available in a tape-recorded test.

There are two other techniques which might be used to test spoken grammar: translation from English into the foreign language and foreign-language-only testing of the pattern practice type.

An experimental speaking test developed by Pimsleur in the early

1960's (Pimsleur, 1961) contained a section in which the student was instructed to listen to a short English sentence and then immediately "convey" the sentence into the foreign language. For example, the English sentence "They saw three friends yesterday" was to be immediately rendered aloud by the student as "Ils ont vu trois amis hier" as a test of the formation of the past indefinite tense. Pimsleur emphasized the term "convey" rather than "translate" and insisted that "the sentences were selected in such a way that they merely provide an input of information, which information must then be transmitted in French" (p. 474).

Most of the sentences in the Pimsleur test were not strictly diagnostic in that they incorporated more than one problem element. ("But Roger hadn't seen them," for example, would involve the student's knowledge of the pluperfect tense, the appropriate direct object for "them," use of the proper negative, and so forth.) However, the same technique could be used in a more diagnostic way by presenting simplified sentences containing only one linguistic problem. Here is an example of a sentence intended to test formation of the third person plural of the irregular French verb *aller*:

(Translate the English sentence into French:)
Peter and Mary are going to school.

"Pierre et Marie vont à l'école."

Diagnostic interest would center on the student's ability to produce the form /võ/. The continuation "à l'école" would not be at issue; indeed, in developing the test, it would be necessary to make sure that "à l'école" and similar peripheral aspects of the test sentence would pose no problem to the student taking the test.

Translation from the native language offers considerable flexibility in the type and range of grammatical points that can be tested, but the teacher may feel that this advantage does not outweigh the use of English as a testing technique. A testing format of the "pattern practice" type offers a means of testing spoken grammar without recourse to the native language. The general procedure is to present (visually) a model sentence together with a partial sentence which the student is asked to complete on the basis of the model. For example:

(Figure out the appropriate word to insert in the blank space and then say the sentence aloud.)

Paul *parle* français.
Nous _____ français.

"Nous parlons français."

This item type effectively highlights the specific element tested and also provides the student all of the non-tested components of the sentence, which he merely reads aloud from the test paper.

In some instances, it is necessary to present a correctly answered example in addition to the model sentence in order to make the student's task sufficiently clear:

> Voilà *mon passeport.*
> Où est *celui* de Jeanne?

Voilà *ma maison.*
Où est _____ de Jeanne?

"Où est celle de Jeanne?"

A potential danger in the use of the "pattern practice" technique is to provide too explicit a cue as to the nature of the expected answer. For example, in the preceding item the presence of *celui* in the example sentence may alert the student to the fact that some pronoun on the order of *ceux, celle,* and so forth is being tested. If the student has studied the various possible forms in an earlier lesson but has not learned the conditions under which each is used, he might nonetheless be able to "guess" *celle* correctly, since he would be mentally selecting from a limited number of possible alternatives.

GENERAL ACHIEVEMENT SPEAKING TESTS

Tests of general achievement provide the student the opportunity to speak at greater length and on "freer" topics than is the case in diagnostic testing. Specific details of pronunciation, vocabulary, and syntax are not formally evaluated, although they do enter into the final test score on a global basis.

A useful distinction can be made between "monologue" speech—in which the student is asked to discourse at some length and without interruption on a particular topic—and "conversational" speech—in which the student engages in a dialogue either with the tape recorder or with a human interlocutor. We will first discuss testing procedures to elicit speech of the monologue type and will later outline considerations in the testing of conversational speech.

SELECTION OF TEST TOPICS FOR "MONOLOGUE" TESTS

We will consider a "topic" to consist of the spoken, written, or pictorial materials (or combination of materials) which present and define the student's speaking task and on the basis of which he makes his response. Topics are often in the form of printed instructions to the student along such lines as "Describe what a person must do to mail a letter. Assume that he has just finished writing it, and describe all the necessary steps from that point." Topics can also be presented through a panel of pictures with associated instructions such as "Relate the story told by the pictures." Regardless of the format involved, speaking test topics should be planned with several important considerations in mind, as described in the following checklist.

1) In what tense(s) will the student be required to speak? Depending on the topic set, the student may be required to speak exclusively or predominantly in present, future, or past tenses. The teacher may wish to set two or three topics, each requiring use of a particular verbal time.

2) In what person(s) will the student be expected to respond? Biographically oriented topics will usually elicit responses in the first-person singular, while requests for descriptions of various sorts will tend to produce third-person (singular or plural) responses. Again, the teacher may consider it appropriate to test the student's ability to speak correctly in a number of persons, and different topics can be designed for this purpose.

3) What vocabulary areas should be emphasized? The teacher should not present topics which require a vocabulary knowledge beyond that encountered by the student during the work of the course. Especially to be guarded against are topics which hinge on one or two specialized words with which the students would probably not be familiar. Depending on their individual approaches to the testing situation, some students may succeed in paraphrasing a crucial vocabulary item (or in some cases, may simply substitute the native-language equivalent) while other students may fall silent and be unable to continue, even though they would be able to give a quite good total performance if they were provided the necessary word. Extent of vocabulary should, of course, comprise one element of the speaking test considered globally, but the student's knowledge

or lack of knowledge of individual words should not be allowed to influence unduly his performance on an entire test section.

4) Would the topic be difficult for a native speaker of the language? Many teachers have a tendency to propose speaking (and writing) topics which place a premium on the student's ability to follow a specific train of logic, to marshal arguments on one side or another or, in general, to deal intellectually with the subject matter. Native speakers vary widely in their ability to perform tasks of this sort, without regard to their obviously satisfactory ability to use the language for normal communication purposes. On the general assumption that tests of foreign-language achievement should not require the student to surpass the capacities of the average native speaker of that language, tests of general speaking ability should be limited to rather commonplace topics which can be successfully answered by any student possessing the requisite linguistic capabilities, regardless of his level of proficiency in exposition, analysis, and the like.

5) Is the topic sufficiently delimited that all students will give reasonably similar responses? If the speaking topic is so generally phrased that students take widely different approaches in their answers, scoring difficulty is increased considerably. For example, if students are asked to "describe their most interesting experience," the responses obtained can be expected to have very little comparability in topical area or vocabulary. Students whose "most interesting experience" was a rather easily described event will be able to respond to the test question much more readily and effectively than students who valiantly struggle through a genuinely complicated tale. In scoring such a topic, the teacher would either tend to accord higher scores to students with "easier" descriptions or face the almost impossible task of making suitable allowances the inherent difficulty of the different descriptions.

EXAMPLE TOPICS

It is difficult to give examples of suitable speaking topics without knowing the instructional history of the group to be tested. The following may give a general idea of topics that would be appropriate near the end of a typical beginning course.

1) Describe the things you did *yesterday,* from the time you got up in the morning until the end of the school day. Give as much detail as you can. (The intent here is to have the student speak in the past tense and to use first-person singular forms. Vocabulary emphasis would be on typical daily activities such as washing, eating

breakfast, etc., and would also include school-related lexicon—classes, school subjects, schedules, and so forth. It is assumed, of course, that vocabulary appropriate to these areas would have been taught at some point in the course. Although this topic does ask for biographical information, it would be expected that most students would have had comparable daily routines and that their responses would thus be generally similar in content.)

2) Describe the job of a waitress from the time a customer enters a restaurant until the time he leaves. (This topic emphasizes use of third-person, present-tense discourse. General vocabulary— "food," "serve," "money," etc.—would permit a minimum level response, and students with a more extensive vocabulary should be able to give a somewhat more elaborate answer. Since the duties of a waitress are well known, specialized information is not required to deal with the topic. The teacher may wish to provide the foreign-language equivalent for "waitress" and "client" to insure that the student will not be hindered by lack of these basic terms.)

It is important to have the student speak on several different topics in a given achievement test. If the entire test is restricted to one or two speech topics, there is a substantial chance that for some reason a particular student will not be able to talk readily on a certain topic even though his overall proficiency is at a high level. By having the student talk for perhaps half a minute or so on five or six different topics, rather than for several minutes on one or two topics, the teacher can avoid the possibility that the student's lack of knowledge of a needed vocabulary item or some other minor difficulty will not have a highly detrimental effect on his total test score. Use of a number of topics also gives the teacher greater opportunity to sample different subject areas and modes of discourse within a single test.

Modalities for "Monologue" Tests

Pictorial materials can be used to advantage in presenting speaking topics of the "monologue" type. The student can either be given a single picture which he is asked to describe in detail or a set of pictures depicting a series of events which he is to relate. Considerable control of structure and lexicon can be exercised in this way, but since the student is constrained to speak solely on the content of the pictures, the teacher should make sure that no specialized vocabulary will be required and that the pictures clearly depict the situation or actions to be described.

Topics can also be presented through written or spoken instructions in the foreign or native language. In view of a possible memory problem, spoken instructions (in either language) should be avoided unless the instructions are quite short and can be easily understood and retained by the student. A preferable technique would be to print the instructions on the test paper, and if desired, also read them aloud. In this way, the student will have a constant reminder of the task he is being asked to perform and can refer to the printed instructions as he feels necessary. Any instructions given in the foreign language should be carefully checked to insure that they present no comprehension problem. This is especially important in the speaking test context because the student's entire spoken response hinges on his understanding of the stimulus topic.

CONVERSATION-BASED TESTS

Tape-recorded speaking tests designed for group administration can present stimulus topics of the "monologue" type in a straightforward and satisfactory manner. The presentation of valid *conversational* situations in this way is a somewhat more complicated matter, from both linguistic and technical viewpoints.

One of the most salient aspects of real-life conversation cannot be incorporated into a tape-recorded test: This is the "give-and-take" of natural conversation, in which the form and content of the responses of each interlocutor are modified on the basis of preceding responses. Since in a tape-recorded test the "conversation" of one of the two speakers must be entirely predetermined, there is no way for the student's response to a given taped utterance to alter the nature of the succeeding taped response. Some semblance of a real-life conversation can be obtained provided that the student "follows the script" in his own responses, but if the student answers in an unanticipated (albeit natural) manner, the conversation rapidly becomes illogical and potentially distracting to the student. For example, consider the following exchange: (Tape) "Comment allez-vous aujourd'hui?" (Student) "J'ai mal à la tête." (Tape) "Parfait. Voulez-vous jouer au tennis, alors?"

The possibility of anomalous student responses can be reduced by telling the student in advance how the conversation is intended to progress. Pimsleur (1961) used this technique in the conversational section of his taped speaking test. Preliminary directions to the student were along the following lines: "We are going to hold a simple, everyday kind of conversation. I want you to imagine that we are both American students who have gone to Paris. We meet there, quite by accident, on the street. We say hello, then I ask you when you got to Paris, and you answer. I ask you where you live, and you tell me that you live with a French family, or in a hotel. Then I ask you what you're doing this evening, and you say you're going to the theater. . . ." (p. 475). Although this technique provides a greater degree of continuity, it is necessarily less realistic than the original "spontaneous" format, since it essentially involves asking the student to say each of a number of previously specified phrases at appropriate points on the tape.[21]

In order to provide more realistic conversational situations, the teacher may wish to restrict tape-recorded procedures to test exercises of the "monologue" type and hold a short face-to-face interview with each student as a measure of his speaking ability in conversational situations.

The general content of a face-to-face interview must be planned as carefully as that of a taped test, and a useful procedure in this regard would be to prepare in advance a number of specific topics, each intended to emphasize a particular type or area of discourse. Although the teacher will of course want to have some flexibility in talking with each individual student (and will also reserve a portion of the allotted interview time for greetings and general pleasantries), he should keep constantly in mind the need to present certain specified stimuli to each student and to listen carefully and analytically to the response made. A scoring form outlining both the topics to be broached and the lexical or grammatical aspects at issue would be helpful both in conducting the interview and in evaluating the student's performance. For psychological reasons, the teacher should attempt to minimize the "test" aspects of the interview and should not make an ostentatious display of scoring forms or similar paraphernalia in the student's presence. For the same reason, any necessary notes should be taken as unobtrusively as possible.

SCORING PROCEDURES

An obvious suggestion for the scoring of a general achievement speaking test would be simply to listen to the entire test and make an overall judgment of the student's performance on a scale such as "excellent," "good," "average," "mediocre," and "poor." Although such

---

21 Delattre (1960) developed a tape-recorded speaking test based in part on a simulated telephone conversation in which the student was instructed by the test tape to convey certain information or to ask certain questions of an imaginary interlocutor (e.g., "Demandez à votre ami s'il est libre cet après-midi"; "Dites-lui que vous ne l'entendez pas très bien.") (p. 79) Again, the inherent artificiality of the taped-test situation may be noted.

a procedure has the advantages of speed and simplicity, it is generally considered that this type of "whole-test" evaluation tends to be somewhat unreliable in the sense that the teacher would be likely to assign different ratings to the students' performances if he were to score the tests on different occasions, or that different teachers would assign different ratings to the same student performance.

Operational statements of the actual linguistic performances expected at each rating level help to define the scale levels more clearly and permit a higher degree of scoring reliability. For example, Valette (1967, p. 83) presents the following six-level scale:

    0 — no response: partial incomprehensible response
    1 — poor: total effort but incomprehensible response
    2 — fair: faulty production but more or less comprehensible
    3 — acceptable: comprehensible but with minor faults
    4 — excellent: but short of perfect
    5 — superior: perfect performance

Using this scale, a score of "poor" (or 1, in numerical terms) is to be given a student who makes a "total effort" but produces an "incomprehensible response;" to obtain a score of "acceptable" (3), the student must speak in a manner that is "comprehensible but with minor faults."

The usefulness of an operationally-based scale of this type is dependent on the ease and directness with which the verbal criteria can be applied to a specific performance. Although the guideline statement "comprehensible but with minor faults" represents an improvement over the simple indication "acceptable," the teacher is still faced with the problem of deciding whether a given performance is "comprehensible" and, if "comprehensible," whether it contains any faults which are more than "minor."

A considerable improvement over scoring schemes based on a global appraisal of the student's performance is the use of separate scales for each of several component aspects of the performance. Specific linguistic areas such as "vocabulary," "pronunciation," "structure," and "fluency" are outlined, and for each area a separate scale is developed. This procedure has the distinct advantage of corresponding more closely to the linguistic realities of typical student performances. For example, a student may show a quite extensive knowledge of vocabulary but have little control of structure; and rather than having to combine both these aspects into a single scoring framework, it becomes possible for the teacher to rate each separately. Furthermore, the use of separate scales allows much greater specificity in the operational statements of performance for the various score levels.

An example of a four-scale system with different scoring categories for each scale is shown below:

Pronunciation:

Phonemically accurate pronunciation throughout	4
Occasional phonemic error, but generally comprehensible	3
Many phonemic errors; very difficult to perceive meaning	2
Incomprehensible, or no response	1

Vocabulary:

Consistent use of appropriate words throughout	4
Minor lexical problems, but vocabulary generally appropriate	3
Vocabulary usually inaccurate, except for occasional correct word	2
Vocabulary inaccurate throughout, or no response	1

Structure:

No errors of morphology or syntax	4
Generally accurate structure, occasional slight error	3
Errors of basic structure, but some phrases rendered correctly	2
Virtually no correct structures, or no response	1

Fluency:

Speech is natural and continuous. Any pauses correspond to those which might be made by a native speaker.	4
Speech is generally natural and continuous. Occasional slight stumblings or pauses at unnatural points in the utterance.	3
Some definite stumbling, but manages to rephrase and continue.	2
Long pauses, utterances left unfinished, or no response.	1

To use a scoring system of this type, the teacher would apply each of the scales separately to each of the topics on the tape-recorded test and/or the face-to-face interview. For example, if the entire speaking test consisted of four separate topics, the teacher would rate the student's performance on the first topic with respect to "pronunciation," "vocabulary," "structure," and "fluency," and then make similar ratings for each of the other topics. The student's final score (in this example) would be the total of 16 different ratings.

The fact that generally-oriented speaking tests are not intended to be highly diagnostic has already been emphasized. Nonetheless, the teacher may wish to examine students' sub-scores for "pronunciation," "vocabulary," and so forth. While a certain degree of useful information may be obtained in this way, it should be borne in mind that such sub-scores may be expected to be considerably less reliable than the total test score, especially when examining the performance of a single student rather than the average performance of the test group as a whole.

READING

The kinds of tests used to measure student achievement in reading vary depending on the particular aspect of the skill which is being evaluated. At the most basic level, "reading" involves visually discriminating the printed characters of the language—a process somewhat analogous to aural discrimination learning in the listening comprehension area. At a somewhat higher level, the student is engaged in attaching semantic meanings to various combinations and positionings of these characters. Activity in this area can be categorized into the two major components of *vocabulary learning* and *grammar learning*, with the former roughly defined as attaching meaning to "root" aspects of printed words, and the latter, as attaching meaning both to morphological changes within the words and to the sequential positioning of these words within the phrase or sentence. A third level, which is quantitatively rather than qualitatively different from the preceding, involves a great increase in the number of lexical items with which the student is familiar, a high level of mastery of grammatical structure, and an associated ability to grasp nuances of word selection and phraseology, to understand extended meanings of words, and in general, to derive as much semantic information from a given text as would a native speaker of the language.

CHARACTER RECOGNITION

Learning problems at the first, or writing system, level are relatively slight for students of French, Italian, and Spanish, since all three incorporate—with a few minor exceptions such as the French c-cedilla—the Roman alphabet familiar to native speakers of English. These alphabetical "exceptions," together with a few different extra-alphabetical conventions (such as inverted question marks and exclamation points in Spanish) require little explicit instruction, and are thus not usually the objects of formal teaching or testing.

On the other hand, the recognition of both German script characters and the non-Roman characters of Russian does present some difficulty for the beginning student and acccordingly constitutes a genuine instructional and measurement concern. Tests of the recognition of German script characters can be designed to check whether the student can "see through" the printing style of such letters as j, ſ, ſ, b, þ to recognize the normal Roman characters which they represent. A straightforward procedure in this respect would be to present a number of printed German script letters and to ask the student to write the appropriate Roman equivalent in each case. For example:

(Write the Roman letter corresponding to the German script letter.)

A multiple-choice item type might also be used in which the student would see a single script letter and would choose one of several Roman options, as shown below:

(Mark the Roman letter corresponding to the German script letter.)

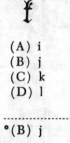

    (A) i
    (B) j
    (C) k
    (D) l

    *(B) j

Multiple-choice items of this type would not give precise diagnostic information because of the chance success factor and would also be more difficult to prepare. Thus, wherever administratively possible, use of the free-response technique would be preferred.

Testing the recognitional knowledge of Russian characters is a somewhat different matter, since the student's task is not to identify Roman alphabet equivalents in a specialized typeface but rather to distinguish a number of different alphabetical characters among themselves within the framework of the Russian writing system. If the student is given a large amount of time to make these discriminations, virtually perfect results can be anticipated, since the characters are sufficiently different to allow them to be discriminated easily on close examination. However, fluency in reading Russian requires that the necessary discriminations be made quite rapidly, and the student's ability to do this can be determined by a speeded test in which the student is asked to circle or cross out each of several appearances of a given character in various words or strings of characters:

(Circle the letter *л* each time it appears in the words below. Work as rapidly as you can.)

или лагерь нашли июль
фотографировать линия
целовали гид орфография
сломал агрессивный милый
уничтожили уничтожения
поспешил могучий господин
организация много мгновение

Any actual test would of course include a large number of items of this type, each based on a different character. To preserve the diagnostic value of the test, the student's work on each character would have to be timed and scored separately.

It should be noted that these and similar character discrimination tests involve only a *recognitional* response by the student. The student's ability to form the target-language characters properly would constitute a test of *productive* (writing) ability and would have no bearing on reading comprehension as such.

READING VOCABULARY

A straightforward and highly diagnostic procedure for testing the student's knowledge of reading vocabulary is simply to have him say or write English equivalents for the words in question. However, this technique is not without serious criticism by many members of the profession. Valette (1967) has cautioned that "It is particularly inadvisable to reinforce the dangerous tendency to establish word-for-word equivalents between English and the target language" by using English in vocabulary test items (p. 124). Brooks, in a test review appearing in the sixth edition of the *Mental Measurements Yearbook* (Buros, ed., 1965), criticized the "matching of isolated words in the manner of a bilingual dictionary" as one of the "peda-gogical misdeeds which early levels of language teaching and testing cannot too soon renounce" (p. 402). These and similar criticisms notwithstanding, the use of English responses must be considered the only strictly diagnostic technique available for the testing of reading vocabulary. The other possible response modalities may all be ruled out for one or more reasons. Multiple-choice responses (of whatever sub-type) are affected by the chance response factor and the possibility of peripheral linguistic clues. The "non-English" free-response modalities, "spoken foreign language" and "written foreign language," are subject to diagnostic contamination through skills mixing. In testing situations using either of these response modalities, the student would have to give a close synonym, para-phrase, or definition of the tested word in order to demonstrate com-prehension. Students who were able to make such a response could be considered unambiguously to understand the meaning of the word, but the reverse would not be true since it would not be possible to determine absolutely whether lack of knowledge of the tested word or an insufficiently high level of speaking or writing ability was responsible for a faulty response (or lack of response).

Modalities which avoid the use of English and which can be used for the "suggestive"—although not perfectly diagnostic—testing of reading vocabulary include "written foreign language," "spoken foreign language," and multiple-choice formats of the "pictorial" and "FL reading" type. As discussed in the preceding paragraph, the skills mixing involved in the use of written or spoken foreign-language responses may make these techniques unsuitable for students at the lower levels; for more advanced students, however, paraphrase or definition items using these response modalities may be found appro-priate.

"Pictorial" multiple-choice items to test reading vocabulary may take a form such as the following:

(Select the picture corresponding to the printed word.)

coude

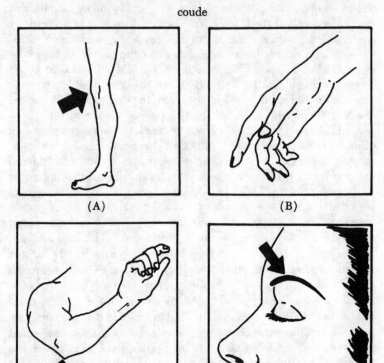

(A)   (B)

(C)   (D)

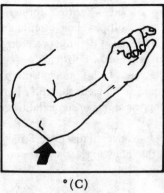

*(C)

Alternatively, the tested word may be used in a short sentence rather than being presented in isolation. In this case, the sentence context should not provide any clue to the correct picture. As previously discussed, the chief limitation of this technique is that it does not permit the testing of the many lexical items which cannot be represented through pictures. The remaining response modality—"multiple-choice FL reading"—must be adopted in these instances. Several different item types may be produced from this basic format, as shown in the following examples:

(Select the word which is most appropriately associated with the underlined word.)
  Il s'assied.

> (A) chaise
> (B) tableau
> (C) mur
> (D) fenêtre

°(A) chaise

This type of item has the advantage of being very quickly written, and it also minimizes the possibility that the student will guess the meaning of the tested word on the basis of peripheral linguistic clues. A major drawback is that the format is not very realistic from a language-use point of view. Also, unless care is taken to keep the conceptual relationship between the tested word and the answer options as simple and as straightforward as possible, an intelligence or "puzzle-solving" element may be introduced.

(Select the most appropriate completion of the sentence.)
  Pierre voulait se désaltérer parce qu'il avait. . . .

> (A) faim
> (B) tort
> (C) raison
> (D) soif

°(D) soif

It is assumed in this type of item (and also in the preceding) that the student will not have any difficulty understanding either the answer options or the material surrounding the tested word, so that if he does in fact know the word he will have no difficulty marking his response. The teacher should also make sure the context in which the word is presented does not provide linguistic clues to the correct response. In the example above, the context is essentially neutral since from the information provided in the sentence (excluding the tested word), the student would have no hint as to which of the answer options was the most appropriate. A longer, "giveaway" context such as "Pierre voulait se désaltérer d'une bonne boisson parce qu'il avait. . . ." would permit the student to answer the item correctly even though he did not know the meaning of *se désaltérer*.

To check for the presence of peripheral clues, the teacher can prepare a special version of the test in which each of the "tested" words is blacked out or concealed. This test is then shown to a person competent in the foreign language who attempts to answer each item on the basis of the remaining context. If the correct answer cannot be guessed when the "tested" word is concealed, the context may be considered neutral.

(Select the most appropriate completion of the sentence.)
L'endroit le plus élevé d'une montagne s'appelle le. . . .
    (A) point
    (B) sommet
    (C) chef-d'oeuvre
    (D) panorama

----
  *(B) sommet

This item type differs from the preceding two in that the "tested" word (*sommet*) appears in the answer options rather than in the item stem. In writing such an item, enough information must be given in the stem to define the tested word unambiguously; but by the same token it becomes possible for the student who knows all of the answer options except the tested word to rule them out as inappropriate and thus arrive at the correct answer. This possibility considerably reduces the diagnostic potential of the item type, although it may be considered useful as a general measure of vocabulary knowledge.

READING GRAMMAR

As is the case with vocabulary testing, "reading grammar" can be tested with a high degree of diagnostic accuracy provided that native-language responses are permitted. Below are a number of French examples based on a written response in English.

(Write the English equivalent of the sentence shown.)
Jacques leur donne un livre.

Jacques gives them a book.

The tested element is the indirect object pronoun *leur,* and the student's response would be considered correct if "them" appears in the written sentence. Other aspects would be ignored (the student could, for example, write either "gives" or "will give" without penalty). Lexicon is deliberately held at a very low level of difficulty since it is simply used to convey the grammatical point at issue. Alternatively, the word *leur* could be underlined in the stimulus sentence, and the student could be asked to translate only the underlined word. The same item type can be used to test a number of other grammatical elements:

(Write the English equivalents of the sentences shown.)
Il préfère celui-là.

He prefers that one.

Que voyez-vous?

What do you see?

Elle achètera une voiture.

She will buy a car.

Il avait lu le journal.

He had read the paper.

As previously emphasized, the context in which the tested element appears should not in itself give any clue to the appropriate response. For example, "Que voyez-vous dans le réfrigérateur?" could not reasonably refer to a person, and the correct response "what?" would be rather clearly suggested to the student. By the same token, "Elle achètera une voiture la semaine prochaine" would strongly point out the correct response even if the student were unable to recognize the future tense aspect of the verb.

Multiple-choice items can be devised by providing a number of printed English options rather than having the student write his response. For example, the "Il avait lu le journal" item could be rewritten:

(Select the appropriate English equivalent of the printed sentence.)

Il avait lu le journal.
    (A) He read the newspaper.
    (B) He will have read the newspaper.
    (C) He will read the newspaper.
    (D) He had read the newspaper.

----

   *(D) He had read the newspaper.

In addition to introducing a chance success factor, these multiple-choice items are much more difficult and time-consuming to write than the corresponding free-response items; and since the latter can be scored accurately and almost as rapidly by the teacher, there would be little advantage in using them for classroom testing.

It should be pointed out that the often-used "completion" type of item—in which the student selects the grammatically correct form to be inserted in a particular sentence context—is not a test of reading ability as such, but rather an indirect test of writing ability. Consider, for example, the following French item:

(Select the appropriate word to complete the sentence.)
    Hier, Robert et Pierre sont _____ à la plage.
    (A) allés
    (B) allé
    (C) allée
    (D) allées

----

   *(A) allés

Exercises of this type may be considered to reflect a skill used in writing, in which the student must "think of" (and then use) an appropriate form for a given context. This ability is not, however, at issue in reading comprehension: since reading texts always present contextually correct forms, the student's task is simply one of understanding the meaning of the form provided.

TESTS OF GENERAL READING COMPREHENSION

Tests of general reading comprehension are analogous in many respects to those of listening comprehension. The overall technique is to provide a number of printed passages containing, for the most part, elements of grammar and lexicon which the student would have encountered during the course, and to pose multiple-choice questions on the informational content of the passages. Passage-selection and item-writing suggestions are similar to those already discussed for tests of general listening comprehension and for that reason will be summarized only briefly here.

1) Passages should represent a real use of the written language and would preferably be drawn or adapted from a genuine foreign-language source.

2) The type of discourse should be one with which the student has had some acquaintance during the course, rather than a novel genre presented for the first time in the test situation.

3) A few elements of unfamiliar vocabulary or grammar may be retained provided that they are not crucial to the comprehension of major portions of the passage or to the answering of a particular test item. Vocabulary or grammar which is "crucial" in this sense should be simplified or paraphrased as appropriate.

4) The content of the passage should not be familiar to the student through outside knowledge.

5) The passage length and the number of items per passage should be carefully correlated in order to avoid the undesirable extremes of presenting sizeable amounts of written material on which no questions are based, or of asking questions on minor points as a result of too heavy "mining" of a relatively short passage.

6) The items should be written in conformance with the basic item-writing pointers discussed, including: length and parallelism of answer options, level of generality of options, "distractive" power of incorrect options, and independence of items when used in sets.

Since in a reading comprehension test the entire printed passage is constantly available to the student as he works through the test questions, the "memory factor" associated with listening comprehension tests does not apply. However, this should not be taken as an opportunity to write test questions on minor points of detail in the passage or, especially, to test the student's familiarity with specific lexical items. Other more straightforward and accurate techniques are available for this purpose, and it is quite uneconomical of time and effort to locate, edit, and reproduce general comprehension passages simply as a vehicle for testing vocabularly knowledge. Furthermore, there is a substantial possibility that a lexical item appearing in a particular reading passage will be tested simply "because it is there" and not because the teacher has any more fundamental reason to select it for testing.

The above caution against testing vocabulary in a general comprehension test refers only to situations in which the student must recall the word from memory, that is, when the passage itself does not provide a substantial indication of its meaning. The ability to *infer* the meaning of nouns or other lexical elements on the basis of contextual clues is a highly important aspect of overall reading ability and as such merits inclusion in a general comprehension test. This can often be accomplished by asking a question on a lexical item which the student would *not* be expected to know from prior acquaintance but whose general meaning could be inferred from the passage context. For example, in the French sentence, "Georges avançait avec peine dans l'obscurité, butant contre les pierres sur son chemin et tombant dans les trous," the term *butant* could be the object of a test question, not for its own sake but to check whether the student were able to integrate a sufficient number of linguistic clues within the surrounding sentence to understand quite clearly its informational content.[22] A possible item would be:

Selon le passage, nous savons que Georges
(A) a cherché des pierres pour s'orienter.
(B) a marché sur des pierres.
(C) a soulevé avec peine des pierres.
(D) a perdu l'équilibre à cause des pierres.

----

*(D) a perdu l'équilibre à cause des pierres.

----

[22] The example sentence is taken from Siebert and Crocker (1958), used by permission of Harper and Row, publishers. The authors provide an extensive corpus of French sentences and longer passages containing low-frequency words whose general meaning may be inferred from context.

In addition to questions on the strict informational content of a given passage, general comprehension tests often include items intended to determine the student's appreciation of the overall style or tone of the passage, the presence of humor or irony, the personality and feelings of the protagonists, and so forth. Although the ability to make rather subtle appreciations of this sort is a valid aspect of reading comprehension, especially at the higher levels of proficiency, the attainment of this skill is difficult to measure through multiple-choice techniques because of a technical difficulty that can be referred to as the "odd adjective" problem. Assume, for example, that on the basis of various indications in a printed dialogue, one of the two speakers can clearly be seen as "insincere." In order to test the student's appreciation of this situation, the natural item-writing procedure would be to set up a test question about the speaker's attitude which would have "insincere" (or a similar expression) as its key. The draft item might read as follows:

On the basis of the passage, we can judge that the second speaker is
(A)
(B) insincere
(C)
(D)

A problem now arises in trying to find incorrect options to complete the item. Adjectives close in meaning to "insincere" cannot be used because they would come dangerously close to being considered acceptable answers themselves. Terms such as "devious," "deceitful," or even "guarded" would have to be rejected for this reason, and options considerably less close in meaning to the correct answer would be required. "Frank," "candid," and "open" would all meet this requirement, and would result in the following set of options:
(A) frank
(B) insincere
(C) candid
(D) open
This exemplifies the "odd adjective" problem in that all of the options are semantically close in meaning except for the single correct option. A perceptive student would be able to determine that option B is the intended answer by reasoning that the other options are virtually equivalent but cannot be simultaneously correct; and by this token, they may all be ruled out in favor of the single "odd" option. The

problem could be remedied somewhat by finding a more neutral term for one of the incorrect options (such as "noncommital" instead of "open"), but an alert student would still be able to rule out "frank" and "candid" as probable answers.

The "odd-adjective" difficulty can be avoided, although at the expense of multiple-choice format, by having the student write short English sentences in response to questions on mood, style, passage tone, *sous-entendus,* and the like. If the student is asked to respond briefly and concisely, the teacher should be able to score questions of this type with reasonable speed and convenience.

WRITING

An initial student activity in learning to "write" involves learning to form properly the alphabetic characters or other visual symbols of the language. For students of common European languages such as French, German, Italian, and Spanish, direct transfer of long-standing and thoroughly trained character-writing habits in the native language makes "learning" of the written symbols of the target language unnecessary for the most part. The student of Russian faces a more difficult problem, since many of the written characters of the Russian alphabet are entirely novel or are formed somewhat differently from the English equivalents. Students of Arabic as well as of Chinese and other languages having non-alphabetic writing systems must go through a long period of training in forming the symbols of the language correctly before they can begin to use them in writing meaningful phrases.

CHARACTER FORMATION

Testing procedures appropriate at the character-forming stage include simple *copying,* in which the student attempts to reproduce written models as closely as possible, and at a somewhat later point, *rapid copying* in which the student copies the material as quickly as possible while maintaining legibility. Valette (1967) suggests that in grading student performance on a non-speeded copying test, the teacher should be "extremely strict in demanding a perfect copy" (p. 138). Although close attention to detail may be a useful principle for teaching purposes, a more valid test of the student's ability to form characters in an acceptable manner would be to have another teacher, without seeing the original models, attempt to identify the symbols intended by the student in each instance. Speeded copying tests could adopt a similar criterion of acceptability: in this case, the student's score would be the number of legible (comprehensible) characters written within a fixed amount of time. Alternatively, the teacher may wish to adopt a strict standard of accuracy in grading a non-speeded exercise and use a simple legibility criterion for tests of rapid copying.

LEXICON AND MORPHOLOGY

A second task in learning to write in the foreign language is that of learning to "spell" words or phrases correctly, in terms of both lexical and morphological accuracy. In order to test the student's attainment of these competencies in a diagnostic manner, it is necessary to provide a formal stimulus of some sort for which the only correct response is the word or phrase in question. Stimuli in English can be used to good effect by presenting short English sentences which the student is asked to translate or "convey" into the target language. For example, "Marie fell off the ladder" would be written by the student as "Marie est tombée de l'échelle." In scoring an item of this type, attention would be paid only to the correct spelling of the verb form (assuming this would be the point tested), and other aspects of the sentence would be ignored. Thus, the student could write "Marie est tombée dessous l'échelle" or "Marie est tombée du laddaire" and receive full credit for proper formation of the tested element.

The presentation of an entire sentence for translation avoids the mixing of native language and target language at a less-than-complete-phrase level, as is the case in "hybrid" test items such as

"Marie _____ de l'échelle."
(fell)

Pictorial stimuli make it possible to avoid use of the native language entirely but are again quite limited in terms of the lexical and morphological aspects that can be presented. Certain concrete nouns can be tested in this way, as can various verbs of action, as shown in the example below:

(On the basis of the picture, write the word which appropriately completes the sentence.)

La muchacha _____ la escalera.

----
sube

Considerably greater flexibility in item writing can be obtained by using written foreign-language stimuli alone. A useful technique for testing a number of prepositions, conjunctions, and other short "function words" is to provide an incomplete sentence for which the desired word would be the only proper completion. For example:

(Write in a single word which correctly completes the sentence.)
Dites-moi ce _____ vous pensez de ma nouvelle robe.

----
que

Allí por _____ menos no hace frío.

----
lo

Even greater flexibility is afforded by item formats which, in addition to presenting an incomplete sentence, provide a completed model as a further guide to the desired response. Many different written elements can be tested in this way, including definite and indefinite articles, descriptive, possessive, and demonstrative adjectives, and various verb forms. For example:

(On the basis of the model, write in a single word which correctly completes the sentence.)

Hier ist mein Vater.
Hier ist _____ Mutter.

----

meine

Donne-moi ce papier!
Donne-moi _____ lettre!

----

cette

Este libro es verde.
_____ sombreros son verdes.

Estos

Compramos un carro.
Compramos _____ blusas.

----

unas

Pensamos en la fiesta.
Tú _____ en la fiesta.

----

piensas

Alain va chez lui.
Il faut qu'Alain _____ chez lui.

----

aille

Written elements which cannot be effectively presented through any of the above question types may often be tested by means of a somewhat more elaborate format in which a correctly answered sample is provided along with the test item:

(On the basis of the model, write in a single word which correctly completes the sentence. Study the sample item beforehand.)

> Je vois ma maison.
> Je *la* vois.

Je connais bien Jean-Claude.
Je _____ connais bien.

----

le

> Voilà mon livre.
> Où est *celui* de Robert?

Voilà mes gants.
Où sont _____ de Marie?

----

ceux

> Salen temprano.
> *Salían* temprano.

Son las once.
_____ las once.

Eran

The item types discussed up to this point are aimed at the diagnostic testing of the student's ability to produce a single written element in a highly specific situation. Because the responses are very short and can be evaluated on a simple right-wrong basis, test scoring is rapid and scoring reliability is extremely high.

In view of the administrative and technical advantages of these "fill-in" writing test formats, there would be considerable interest in determining the extent to which student performance on tests of this type correlates with overall writing ability as measured by more highly face-valid, but less convenient, tests of general achievement. An indication that the correlation may be fairly low arises from a study reported by Pickett (1968) in which French-speaking students of English were administered "parallel forms" of an English writing test, of which one required the student to translate the entire stimulus sentence and the other, simply to fill in a single word to complete the sentence. It was observed that in many cases the "fill-in" technique tended to mask other writing difficulties which became apparent when the same students were asked to translate the entire sentence; the fill-in procedure thus tended to give a falsely positive impression of their overall competence. Probably the safest approach to the interpretation of the student's performance on "fill-in" tests of the type discussed is to consider that they are rigorously indicative only of the student's ability to produce a certain written form within the linguistic context represented by the test item. Extrapolation to other contexts would be made only on the basis of close linguistic correspondence, empirically derived correlations, or both.

There are a number of other item types which are quite specific with respect to the intended answer but which require the student to deal with more than one language aspect in making his response. Accordingly, these item types have less diagnostic accuracy than the preceding, and are more difficult (and somewhat less reliable) to score because of the need to assign "partial credit" to responses that are correct in one or more aspects but not in their entirety. On the other hand, these question types are somewhat closer to actual writing situations, since they involve a longer and more natural response.

The following is a useful procedure to determine the student's ability to make a number of associated morphological changes within a single sentence:

(Rewrite the model sentence so that the new word fits correctly into the rewritten sentence. Make any necessary changes in the form of the words.)

Quelle est cette belle fleur verte?

_____ arbre _____?

Quel est ce bel arbre *vert?*

Ellos no podían irse porque no habían terminado su trabajo.
Yo _____

Yo *no podía irme porque no había terminado mi trabajo.*

¿Quién era el que no compró nada?

¿ _____ los _____?

¿Quiénes eran los *que no compraron nada?*

It would not be reasonable to score questions of this type on a simple "right"-"wrong" basis because this would conceal performance differences between students who had made only one or two minor errors and those whose responses were much less accurate. One possible scoring technique would be to score separately, on a right-wrong basis, each word involving a morphological change. A one-point deduction would be made for any words which should remain invariant but which are changed by the student.

An item type often referred to as "frozen sentences" represents an intermediary step between carefully controlled writing and freer compositions. The student sees a series of words which he is asked to incorporate, in the order given, into a meaningful sentence:

No / ir / cine / dinero

No puedo ir al cine porque no tengo dinero.

professeur / mauvaise note / plus d'effort / fin de l'école.

Mon professeur m'a dit qu'il me donnera une mauvaise note si je ne fais pas plus d'effort avant la fin de l'école.

The stimulus words should be carefully chosen so as to bring a suitable sentence quickly to mind, and should not constitute any sort of logical puzzle. To control the possible responses more closely, the teacher can instruct the students to answer only in the first person singular or in some other specified person. In view of the various suitable responses that might be given, a 3- or 4-point scoring system based on an overall appraisal of response quality would be suggested, rather than the use of a more detailed key or scoring formula.

GENERAL ACHIEVEMENT TESTS

Tests of general achievement in writing are in large part analogous to general achievement speaking tests. In both cases, the student is given the opportunity to carry out production tasks in the language which are reasonably close to real-life goal activities of the course and which allow him to combine many discrete aspects of achievement into a single test exercise.

Perhaps even more so than in the speaking test situation, there is a tendency for developers of general achievement writing tests to present tasks which are too highly demanding in terms of the logical acumen, organizational ability, and stylistic expertise required, that is, which reflect learning goals for scholastically oriented writing instruction in the student's native language. Most of the "writing" that is done by the average, non-academic native speaker of any language is of a quite limited and routine nature, involving simple notes and memoranda of various sorts, business letters, and predominantly, personal correspondence. In none of these areas are organization, choice of words, and the like of particular moment;

indeed, the essentially pedestrian and non-creative quality of non-academic writing is one of its most striking characteristics.

It would seem unreasonable, except at the college-major or graduate school level of foreign-language study, to expect highly organized, stylistic foreign-language writing on the student's part or, by the same token, to propose this as a valid area for testing. Rather, evaluation of student achievement in learning to write the foreign language would appear more profitably directed toward determining the extent to which he can produce sentences that are lexically and grammatically acceptable and which convey adequately the informational content of typical everyday writing situations.

General achievement tests of writing differ somewhat from their speaking test counterparts in that the student's task is more physically laborious and time-consuming. Whereas a student could conveniently address a fairly large number of different topics in a ten-minute speaking test, work on a similar number of writing topics would require a much longer time and would in addition introduce a serious fatigue factor in the student's approach to the later topics. However, if at least a small number of different writing tasks are not included in the test, there is no possibility to sample the student's performance in different types of writing and in different content areas. A useful compromise might be to include about three different writing topics in a test of class-period length, with no more than one hundred words or so to be written on each. This should not unreasonably burden the student and will at the same time allow for some diversity in the writing tasks presented.

Criteria in the selection of writing topics are in many respects similar to those previously discussed for general speaking tests, and need be only briefly outlined here.

1) The types of discourse and content areas incorporated in the writing test should be limited to those which the student has had the opportunity to practice during the formal work of the course. If classroom writing exercises have been mainly based on third-person discourse (perhaps through assignments asking the student to retell the experiences of the textbook dialogue characters), it would be unreasonable as a measure of classroom-based achievement to set writing topics which require the student to answer in the first-person singular. By the same token, the tense(s) in which the topic will require the student to write should have been introduced and practiced in previous exercises.

2) Some thought should be given to the vocabulary required for a proper response to the test topic. Some students can paraphrase

an unknown word in an acceptable manner or in some other way get around a vocabulary problem, but other students will be taken aback, at considerable expense to their overall performance on the topic. This problem can be largely avoided by making sure that key words required in answering the topic are sufficiently familiar to the students or by deliberately providing these words in the test materials.

3) "Free" topics such as discussions of personal biography, individual vacation plans, and the like should be avoided, not only because some students will modify their account to suit areas of writing strength (rather than "telling it like it is") but also because responses which vary widely in content are extremely difficult to evaluate according to a common standard of quality. An ideal topic in this regard is one which provides a simple overall framework for student responses but which at the same time allows students with a higher level of writing ability to elaborate their replies beyond the minimum required by the topic.

In both speaking and writing tests, the general directions given the students are of the utmost importance to the outcome of the test. Unless the students are clearly aware of the nature of the task and of the way in which their answers will be evaluated, they may adopt widely differing response "sets" which will differentially affect their performance on the test, even though they may have similar overall ability. Students who suspect that accuracy is the most important consideration will tend to labor over their responses, while students who imagine that the teacher is primarily interested in volume will try to get down as many words as possible and will pay somewhat less attention to accent marks, grammatical agreements, and similar details.

In order to avoid problems of this type, instructions to the student should be very detailed and should include the following information: (1) the amount of time available for the test as a whole, or for each topic if separately timed; (2) the approximate number of words expected for each topic, and whether or not additional credit will be awarded for a longer response; (3) the relative weighting to be given to grammatical accuracy, extent of vocabulary, and other factors in arriving at a final score.

Both pictorial stimuli and written stimuli in either the foreign language or the native language can be used to specify writing test topics. In using pictorial stimuli, greater continuity in the students' responses can be obtained if a set of pictures representing a series of actions is provided, rather than a single picture which the student is asked to describe in detail. The following set of pictures might constitute a suitable topic for a lower-level test.

(Write a story based on the pictures shown. Your story should contain no more than about one hundred words, and you will receive no extra credit for a longer response. Your story will be evaluated equally for appropriateness of vocabulary and accuracy of grammar. If in addition to describing the actions taking place you are able to provide other details, feel free to do so. You will have 15 minutes to complete your story.)

In the test directions, the teacher may wish to indicate the person in which the story is to be narrated. If first-person is desired, the student could be told to imagine that he is the person in the first picture. Tense may also be specified by such statements as "Imagine that this story took place yesterday." Future tense narration may be cued by an appropriate written instruction and by adopting a picture format in which planned activities are shown in cartoon-like "balloons."

Written stimuli can also be used to specify topics. For example, the student could be instructed to "Write a letter to your French friend, Marc, telling him that you will be traveling to Europe this summer and would like to spend a weekend with him in Paris. Tell him some of the things you would like to do in Paris and ask him to meet you at the airport if possible."

Considerations in the development of a scoring system for general achievement speaking tests have already been discussed in detail, and most of these apply to the evaluation of written responses. An effective scoring technique is to rate the student's response to each topic according to specified linguistic categories, such as appropriateness of vocabulary, grammatical accuracy, and completeness of response. Performance within each category can be rated on a four- or five-point scale, and these sub-scores can then be added within and across categories to provide a total test score.

To avoid the so-called "halo effect," in which the quality of a student's response to one topic influences the teacher's appraisal of other topics, each topic should be evaluated separately, that is, the teacher should score all of the students' responses to the first topic, then all the responses to the second topic, and so forth. For the same reason, it is also advisable for the teacher to conceal the students' names during the scoring process. If student identification is provided only on the cover page of a stapled test booklet, and if responses to each topic are placed on a separate page, these details can be handled quite efficiently.

Chapter 3
Proficiency Testing

Although the point is often lost sight of in the bustle of daily instruction, foreign-language courses are not (or at least should not be) taught for their own sake but rather in order to provide the student with language tools that can usefully be applied in real-life situations. In this light, classroom instruction is not an end in itself but rather the means through which the student acquires the ability to use the language for certain pragmatic purposes. The reading of foreign-language journals in a field of graduate school specialization represents such a use, as does the reading of novels, plays, and other foreign-language materials for purposes of personal enjoyment. However, by far the most significant real-life use of language competencies, and the one which implicitly if not explicitly receives the greatest emphasis in basic high school and college language programs, is that of *communication* with other speakers of the language in various real-life situations.

LINGUISTIC ABILITY AND COMMUNICATIVE PROFICIENCY

One of the most salient characteristics of real-life language use is the absence of a close and easily determined relationship between sheer linguistic ability—defined in such terms as accuracy of pronunciation, range of vocabulary, accuracy and extent of grammatical control, and so forth—and communicative proficiency—defined as the ability to get a message across to an interlocutor with a specified ease and effect. Only at the two extremes of the linguistic ability scale do the degree of technical mastery of the language and communicative proficiency come into precise conjunction. A student who through some process had developed a command of the foreign language equivalent in all respects to that of an educated native speaker would by the same token have acquired an absolute communicative proficiency in the sense that his behavior in real-life language-use situations of all descriptions would be fully acceptable to native interlocutors from both informational and affective standpoints. On the other hand, a student who was unable to function at all in the foreign language would be found to have no communicative proficiency, leaving aside the very limited sort of "communication" that he might be able to accomplish through gestures or other non-verbal means.

Between these two extremes, linguistic proficiency *per se* and the ability to communicate readily and effectively in real-life situations have a tenuous correlation, attributable to a number of factors. First, the high degree of redundancy of language as it is used in actual communication situations can often safeguard a speaker's message even if the utterance is linguistically faulty. When a native speaker of Spanish announces that he "came to the United States on a sheep," a native speaker of English has no difficulty in deriving the appropriate informational content from the sentence because his reception of the phrase, "I came to the United States on a . . .," together with his knowledge of the real world and the travel possibilities which it permits, allows him mentally to ignore the faulty phoneme and to supply the correct one in its place. Indeed, in continuous meaningful discourse there is such a great amount of redundancy that a given utterance can often be highly defective from a linguistic standpoint and still be comprehensible.

Second, the non-native speaker of the language can himself take certain steps to minimize or bypass areas of linguistic weakness in a given communicative situation. If the speaker does not have available the precise vocabulary needed to convey certain items of information he may be able to communicate adequately through circumlocutions. By carefully selecting the morphology and syntax which he employs, he can often communicate in a highly effective manner without having accurate control of certain grammatical areas.

Third, if communicative proficiency is considered to include what may be described as a "social acceptability" factor, then the situational and interpersonal aspects of real-life communication situations can be considered to introduce a further complicating variable between linguistic ability and communicative effect. Depending on the topic of conversation, its physical location, the degree of acquaintanceship of the two speakers, their relative "status," and a number of other extra-linguistic factors, a given degree of linguistic competence on the part of the non-native speaker may show wide variation in acceptability.

For example, a student spending a year abroad with a foreign-language family might be able to converse in a "socially acceptable" manner with members of the family even though his speech were quite deficient in absolute linguistic terms. Family members would "expect" him to make errors in grammar and vocabulary, to speak slowly and hesitatingly, and they would tend to overlook or take little account of these aspects when conversing with him. By contrast, in other situations and with different interlocutors, the student would need a high degree of linguistic ability in order to communicate in a socially acceptable way. For example, the student would not enjoy the luxury of false starts, long pauses, inaccurate vocabulary, and so forth in speaking to the ticket seller at a busy train station: socially acceptable communication in this context would require direct and accurate statements quickly conveying the necessary information.

The preceding observations lead to a very important concept in the development of proficiency tests aimed at measuring communicative ability: this is that testing procedures based on a determination of the accuracy and extent of a student's linguistic command of the foreign language cannot serve to measure directly his communicative proficiency. Rather, what appear to be needed are work-sample tests of communicative proficiency in which the student's performance is evaluated not on the basis of extent of vocabulary, accuracy of morphology and syntax, excellence of pronunciation, and so forth, but rather in terms of the adequacy with which the student can communicate in specified language-use situations.[1]

---

[1] For additional discussions of the distinction between linguistic ability and communicative proficiency, see Brière (1971), Cooper (1970), and Spolsky (1968).

DIRECT TESTING OF COMMUNICATIVE PROFICIENCY

As of the present time, very few testing procedures have been developed which attempt to measure communicative proficiency in a direct manner. The best known and most thoroughly elaborated of these is a face-to-face interview technique originally developed at and used by the Foreign Service Institute of the U.S. Department of State. This testing procedure, known officially as the "Absolute Proficiency Rating" system and referred to informally as the "FSI interview," is designed for administration to government personnel engaged in or being trained for foreign service in diplomatic, political, economic, or cultural areas, and is intended to measure the adequacy with which the student can be expected to communicate in each of a number of language-use situations.

The FSI Language Proficiency Interview

The general testing technique is as follows. The student sits and converses in comfortable, informal surroundings with either one or two trained examiners who are native speakers of the test language or highly qualified non-natives. Over a period of up to thirty minutes depending on the student's level of proficiency, the examiner(s) engage the student in conversation on a number of topics which vary in content and degree of linguistic sophistication. The first few minutes of the interview are spent in casual, relatively simple conversation on the student's biography, personal interests, hobbies, and similar matters. At a somewhat later stage in the interview (if the student's competence permits) the examiners elicit conversation on various aspects of the student's work assignment: overall responsibilities, typical daily activities, technical problems encountered, and so forth. Toward the end of the interview, the pace and sophistication of the interview are increased substantially to include wide-ranging discussions of political, economic, or sociological topics. If two examiners are present, the interview may be terminated by a so-called "situation" period. One examiner pretends to be a monolingual speaker of English and the other a monolingual speaker of the test language. The latter is then identified as a hotel-keeper, taxi driver, importer, government official, or other person, and the student is asked to serve as interpreter for the "monolingual English" examiner, who needs to rent a hotel room meeting certain requirements, to be driven to a particular location, to import certain items, or so forth. Depending on the student's overall proficiency level, the situation period may be used either to establish whether the student is able to function in the language on a "survival" basis or to explore intensively his ability to communicate effectively in sophisticated language-use situations.

At the conclusion of the interview, the student's total performance is rated as corresponding to one of five levels of communicative proficiency: the meaning of each level is defined by fairly detailed verbal descriptions of the kinds of language-use situations in which the student is considered able to function appropriately. A student who is rated at the first level of communicative proficiency (designated level "1") would be expected to be able to "survive" in the foreign-language country in that he would have a communicative ability sufficient to express basic personal needs and to meet elementary courtesy requirements. At the next higher level of proficiency (level "2"), the student would be considered capable of handling "limited work requirements" in his field of employment and of participating in casual conversations on everyday topics. Additional categories are defined up to level "5" which represents proficiency "equivalent to that of an educated native speaker."[2]

The verbal definitions of competence corresponding to each of the rating levels are shown in Table 5.

---

[2] Each numerical rating (except "5") may also be modified by a "plus" to indicate that the student substantially exceeds the requirements for that level but fails to meet the requirements of the next higher level. A rating of "0+" may also be given, indicating that the student can produce a few words in the language but fails to meet the basic "survival" criteria of level "1".

TABLE 5.   FSI ABSOLUTE LANGUAGE PROFICIENCY RATINGS

ELEMENTARY PROFICIENCY (Level 1)
Able to satisfy routine travel needs and minimum courtesy requirements.

Can ask and answer questions on topics very familiar to him; within the scope of his very limited language experience can understand simple questions and statements, allowing for slowed speech, repetition or paraphrase; speaking vocabulary inadequate to express anything but the most elementary needs; errors in pronunciation and grammar are frequent, but can be understood by a native speaker used to dealing with foreigners attempting to speak his language; while topics which are "very familiar" and elementary needs vary considerably from individual to individual, any person at the S-1 level should be able to order a simple meal, ask for shelter or lodging, ask and give simple directions, make purchases, and tell time.

LIMITED WORKING PROFICIENCY (Level 2)

Able to satisfy routine social demands and limited work requirements.

Can handle with confidence but not with facility most social situations including introductions and casual conversations about current events, as well as work, family, and autobiographical information; can handle limited work requirements, needing help in handling any complications or difficulties; can get the gist of most conversations on non-technical subjects (i.e., topics which require no specialized knowledge) and has a speaking vocabulary sufficient to express himself simply with some circumlocutions; accent, though often quite faulty, is intelligible; can usually handle elementary constructions quite accurately but does not have thorough or confident control of the grammar.

MINIMUM PROFESSIONAL PROFICIENCY (Level 3)

Able to speak the language with sufficient structural accuracy and vocabulary to participate effectively in most formal and informal conversations on practical, social, and professional topics.

Can discuss particular interests and special fields of competence with reasonable ease; comprehension is quite complete for a normal rate of speech; vocabulary is broad enough that he rarely has to grope for a word; accent may be obviously foreign; control of grammar good; errors never interfere with understanding and rarely disturb the native speaker.

FULL PROFESSIONAL PROFICIENCY (Level 4)

Able to use the language fluently and accurately on all levels normally pertinent to professional needs.

Can understand and participate in any conversation within the range of his experience with a high degree of fluency and precision of vocabulary; would rarely be taken for a native speaker, but can respond appropriately even in unfamiliar situations; errors of pronunciation and grammar quite rare; can handle informal interpreting from and into the language.

NATIVE OR BILINGUAL PROFICIENCY (Level 5)

Speaking proficiency equivalent to that of an educated native speaker.

Has complete fluency in the language such that his speech on all levels is fully accepted by educated native speakers in all of its features, including breadth of vocabulary and idiom, colloquialisms, and pertinent cultural references.

(Extracted from Circular, "Absolute Language Proficiency Ratings," November 1968, Foreign Service Institute, Washington, D.C.)

It will be useful to consider the extent to which a testing procedure of the FSI type can be considered to fulfill important requirements of a "direct observation" proficiency test. The intent will not be to identify particular shortcomings in the FSI test itself, but rather to point out the theoretical and technical problems involved in direct proficiency testing generally.

SITUATIONAL REALISM OF THE TEST PROCEDURE

A first requirement is that the testing procedure should parallel as closely as possible the situations in which the language competence is manifested in real life. An ideal procedure in this respect would be to transport the student to the restaurant, train station, business office, or other situation in which his communicative ability is at issue, and then to observe and listen to his performance. Practical considerations rule out such an approach in most testing situations, and the alternative thus becomes one of approximating the real-life situation as closely as possible consistent with administrative feasibility.

The fact that the FSI interview does involve a rather extensive face-to-face conversation with native or near-native speakers represents a considerable step toward situational realism of the test procedure. Unlike a tape-recorded speaking test of the usual classroom type, the FSI interview allows for the visual cues and verbal interactions characteristic of real-life conversation. However, the interview conversation cannot be considered a completely accurate replica of the real-life situation for a number of reasons. First, the test surroundings are not those of the restaurant or work location, and the student is thus not free to use props that would be available in the real-life situation to assist him in his communication endeavors. He cannot, for example, point to a menu item or pick up a tool in order to convey his communication intent. Second, and more significantly, the interlocutors with whom the student is asked to speak are at best only reasonable surrogates for the waiters, business associates, or other persons with whom the student would be dealing in the real-life situations in question. Although the examiners can play the role of such persons (and in fact do so in the "situation" portion of the interview), they are unlikely to have sufficient informational background or personal experience to carry out a highly realistic performance. Third, the social and psychological aspects of the interview are necessarily quite different from those present in the real-life situations represented. The relationships of waiter-customer, employer-employee, friend-friend, and so forth are quite different from that of tester-examinee, and these differences would be expected to have a certain effect on the nature and course of the communication.

It is difficult to imagine how these problems could be entirely resolved, even using exceptional means. One could propose a testing room which could be outfitted with various props and furnishings, equipped with a one-way observation mirror, and so on, in which the student and an interlocutor would engage in conversation, but such an arrangement would still be patently artificial and would perhaps increase rather than reduce the "test" aspects of the situation.

Another quasi-realistic situational testing procedure has recently been developed by Educational Testing Service for use in a language evaluation project being carried out for the Peace Corps. The student is given a sheet of paper on which are described, in English, a series of communicative assignments which he must carry out. For example, he may be told that he is to approach a "city health officer" (played by a tester) and to tell the officer that: 1) several villagers have become ill after eating at a traditional feast, 2) three of the villagers have been incapacitated as a result, 3) a Peace Corps vehicle is available to transfer these persons to the local hospital if the officer will authorize payment of medical expenses from city emergency funds.

An interesting aspect of this procedure is that the role-playing tester is not aware in advance of the content of the student's message. At the end of the communication situation, the tester relates to a second tester what he understood the content of the message to be; this is compared for accuracy to the student's original assignment. An important feature of this technique is that it requires the student himself to motivate the conversation, rather than simply to reply to conversational questions. Nonetheless, the overall situation is still rather artificial, and the necessity for the student to refer to his list of "assignments" throughout the course of the conversation is an additional distracting factor.

It appears necessary to conclude that complete situational realism can never be obtained in a formal proficiency test; for this reason, there will always be the possibility of a discrepancy between student performance on the test and his performance in the real-life situations which the test is intended to represent. The magnitude of this discrepancy cannot be determined using experimental or statistical means, but can only be estimated through close observational and logical comparison of the "real-life" and "test" situations.

Considerations in Proficiency Test Scoring

A second important consideration in the development of a valid and useful language proficiency test is that of the scoring procedure adopted. There are two basic criteria which such a procedure should meet. First, the scoring should be based on a direct appraisal of the student's communicative ability rather than on other factors; and second, it should lead to adequately reliable results.

The scoring procedure used in the FSI interview comes reasonably close to fulfilling the first criterion in that the examiner is asked to make his rating of the student's performance on the basis of the verbal descriptions of the proficiency levels, which in themselves constitute statements of the ease and effectiveness with which the student would be considered able to communicate in various language-use situations. For example, in assigning a rating of "1" to a particular student, the examiner would be saying, in effect, that on the basis of the indications of the student's proficiency that he has obtained in the course of the interview, it is his considered opinion that the student is able to "satisfy routine travel needs and minimum courtesy requirements," or more specifically, that he is able to "ask and answer questions on topics very familiar to him," "understand simple questions and statements," "order a simple meal," "ask for shelter or lodging," and so on.

A temptation in the development and use of a communication-defined scoring system, and one which the FSI technique does not avoid completely, is to intermingle statements about desired *linguistic* abilities with the operational statements of communicative competence. For example, the definition of level "2" proficiency includes the statement that a student at this level can "usually handle elementary constructions quite accurately but does not have thorough or confident control of the grammar." It may indeed be the case that a person who can "handle with confidence but not with facility most social situations" would also be able to "handle elementary constructions quite accurately" but would not have a "thorough or confident control of the grammar." Such correspondences should not, however, be assumed *a priori* but should be determined empirically through controlled studies. The mixing of communicative and linguistic criteria in a single testing system or rating scheme serves only to obscure the distinction between the two types of measurement and decrease the validity of the test as a direct measure of communicative proficiency.

Although scoring procedures based directly and exclusively on an appraisal of the student's communicative ability may be considered highly valid, they cannot by the same token be assumed to provide scores which are *reliable* in the sense that differing scores may be considered to reflect only differing degrees of communicative proficiency, and not individual scoring tendencies of the raters.

The term *inter-rater reliability* is used to describe the consistency with which two or more raters assign the same scores to the same test performance. Low inter-rater reliability is a serious problem because this makes it impossible to compare on a common scale student scores assigned by different raters. The degree of inter-rater reliability can be determined by having a number of different raters evaluate the same series of test performances; in an interview situation, this would mean that two or more raters would have to be on hand during each interview and would have to rate the student's performance independently.

Rigorous studies of the inter-rater reliability of the FSI technique have not been reported in the literature, but a small-scale study has been carried out recently at Educational Testing Service in which eighty FSI interviews in French were rated independently by two testers. The "1" to "5" score levels assigned were found to coincide in approximately 95 percent of the cases, indicating a high degree of inter-rater reliability, at least for the two raters involved in the study.

A second aspect of scoring reliability is that of *intra-rater reliability*, which refers to the extent to which a single rater can consistently assign the same score to a given student performance. Statistical checks on intra-rater reliability are carried out by having the tester rate the same set of tests on separate occasions and determining the extent to which the original scores can be duplicated on the subsequent scoring. In paper-and-pencil testing, the determination of intra-rater reliability is a relatively straightforward matter. In a writing test, for example, the student's test booklet would simply be scored initially and then put aside for a period of time until it would be brought out (with the original scoring indications concealed) for a second scoring by the same rater. The situation is somewhat more difficult for a conversation-based interview test, because the interview cannot easily be "reproduced" for a second scoring. A tape recording of the conversation would not be entirely satisfactory, since it would not show expressive visual components of the original interview. Video recording would meet this requirement but would be administratively complicated and probably highly distracting to the tested students.

In regard to the question of how high the scoring reliability of a direct-observation proficiency test should be, the only suitable answer is that it should be as high as possible. High scoring reliability is important not only in the direct utilization of proficiency test results but also in connection with correlational studies comparing the relationship between proficiency test scores and scores on other types of tests. In order for a strong relationship to be shown, the reliabilities of both tests must be quite high.

High scoring reliability should not, however, be obtained at the expense of measurement validity. There is a natural tendency in developing scoring procedures for judgmentally-scored tests to attempt to make these procedures more "objective" by adopting certain simplifying and organizing procedures which will allow scorers to agree more closely on the rating that should be awarded in a given instance. This has happened to a certain extent in the course of active use of the FSI interview. In addition to the basic verbal criteria shown in Table 5, the FSI has developed a chart of "Factors in Speaking Proficiency" which the examiner can use to help him arrive at a final interview rating. This chart consists of a two-way grid with the five official rating levels on one dimension and five linguistic categories—"pronunciation," "grammar," "vocabulary," "fluency," and "comprehension" along the other dimension. Within each cell of this grid, there is a short description of communicative (and in some cases, linguistic) performances pertaining to that category which the student should demonstrate at the designated level of proficiency. For example, a level-"2" performance from the point of view of "grammar" would be one in which the student demonstrates "fair control of most basic syntactic patterns" and "conveys meaning accurately in simple sentences most of the time." A level-"3" performance with respect to "fluency" would be demonstrated by a student whose speech is "rarely hesitant" and who is "always able to sustain conversation through circumlocutions." In using this chart, the tester marks the cell descriptions which he considers to describe most accurately the student's performance in each of the five linguistic categories; the resulting profile is used as an additional guide to the proper overall rating to be assigned.

A drawback in the use of additional scoring aids of this type is that they may lead the rater away from paying close attention to the original performance criteria on which the test is conceptually based. In the FSI case, the purpose of the interview is to determine the student's ability to communicate appropriately in a number of language-use situations; and although accuracy of pronunciation, fluency, extent of vocabulary and so forth would be expected to have a bearing on the final rating in that these aspects would contribute to the overall accuracy and ease of communication, the deliberate categorization and separation of these elements for scoring purposes may obscure in the scorer's mind the original broad criteria on which the score ratings are ultimately based and lead him in some cases to assign a different rating than he would using the official criteria alone.

Implications of the above for the development of proficiency test scoring procedures generally are that attempts to increase the objectivity of the scoring process should not be allowed to jeopardize close adherence to the basic purpose and measurement rationale of the test itself. While high scoring reliability is of course desirable, measurement validity must take precedence in any situations in which the two may be in conflict.

COMMUNICATIVE PROFICIENCY TESTS FOR SCHOOL LANGUAGE PROGRAMS

Development of communicative proficiency tests for use in connection with basic foreign-language courses at the high school or college level would require close consideration of the real-life language-use goals of the instructional program. If the program intended to develop only a "tourist abroad" competence in the language, then language-use situations such as ordering meals, making purchases, asking directions, making travel arrangements, and the like would be appropriately involved. Presumably, most basic foreign-language programs attempt to develop a somewhat more extensive proficiency: the popular textbook theme in which American students spend a year abroad with a foreign family and travel about the country during vacation periods may be indicative of the types of real-life situations toward which a number of teaching programs are implicitly directed.

In addition to specifying the types of language-use situations to be included in the test, the test developers would have to consider the degree of emphasis which is placed in these situations on the smoothness, accuracy, and overall naturalness of the student's performance. As previously discussed, sociological and psychological aspects of a particular communicative situation have a strong bearing on the "acceptability" of the communication (for a given level of linguistic competence), and both the testing procedure and the scoring system adopted would have to take these factors into account.

At the present state of the proficiency testing art, it is impossible to provide firm information or even close guesses on the test formats and scoring procedures that could most profitably be used in school-based proficiency testing. All of the formats discussed (straightforward conversation, interpretive "situations," and communicative "assignments") depart in various ways from the real-life situations represented, and other proposed techniques would have to be investigated and their merits weighed from the standpoints of both measurement validity and reliability. In order to accomplish a task of this magnitude, the cooperative efforts of teachers, testing specialists, psychologists, linguists, sociologists, and many other persons would have to be exerted over a considerable period of time, and extensive experimental studies and test administration programs would have to be carried out. In view of the obvious need for direct tests of communicative proficiency as criterion measures of language learning success, the development of such tests should be considered a matter of urgency by both foreign-language teachers and test developers.[3]

CORRELATIONAL APPROACHES TO PROFICIENCY MEASUREMENT

Although proficiency testing procedures of the type described constitute the most direct and most highly face-valid technique for measuring communicative proficiency, the relatively great complexity and expense of administering such tests would probably prohibit their routine use in many school settings. For this reason, there would be considerable practical interest in establishing statistical equivalences between direct proficiency measures and tests of other types which could be more readily and more extensively administered in the schools. Unfortunately, little formal research has been carried out in this regard. Carroll (1967) reported a study in which a total of 127 participants in NDEA summer institutes were administered both the FSI interview and the listening, speaking, reading, and writing portions of the *MLA Proficiency Tests for Teachers and Advanced Students*. Correlations ranging from .58 to .86 were obtained between the FSI ratings and the MLA test scores, indicating a fairly high correspondence between these two types of measures and suggesting the possibility of using MLA test scores to "predict" scores on the FSI interview with a reasonable degree of accuracy.

The author has conducted a currently unpublished study in which

---

[3] A similar appeal has been made by Brière (1971).

FSI scores of 44 Peace Corps trainees in French were correlated with a series of highly objective tests of speaking vocabulary and grammar. Correlations obtained ranged from .82 to .92. In considering results of both of these studies, account should be taken of the relatively small number of cases tested, and of the fact that the examinees were foreign-language teachers and Peace Corps trainees rather than students in typical high school or college language programs. Nonetheless, the substantial correlations found between proficiency test scores and other measures of language achievement in these instances suggest that similar investigations in regular school settings would prove profitable.

In order to carry out such a research program, first attention would have to be given to the proficiency test itself. Although certain portions of the FSI interview may be considered to parallel the instructional goals of basic language courses, a substantial proportion of the interview—including the associated definitions of proficiency—is based on language-use situations typically encountered in government service. A modified FSI interview, or a new type of test explicitly developed for use with school language courses, would provide a more valid criterion against which the more indirect testing procedures could be compared.

The second step would be to conduct extensive testing studies in which large groups of students would be administered both the direct proficiency test and various other measures anticipated to have a high correlation with the proficiency test. Well-known standardized achievement tests such as the *MLA-Cooperative Tests,* the *MLA Proficiency Tests for Teachers and Advanced Students,* and the *Pimsleur Proficiency Tests* would be logical candidates, and experimental tests of various types could also be included.[4] From a language research standpoint, measures showing the highest and most stable correlations with the communicative proficiency test could be carefully analyzed in an effort to elucidate more fully the interrelationships between linguistic ability and communicative competence.

Immediate practical benefits of such a study would be the establishment of expectancy tables or other means through which scores on the indirect measures could be translated into probable scores on the direct proficiency test; in this way, students and teachers could obtain a general idea of the student's level of proficiency in real-life

---

[4] One example is the listening comprehension test with deliberately lowered signal-noise ratio developed by Spolsky *et al.* (1968).

terms even though a direct proficiency test could for some reason not be administered.

The use of correlational procedures is not, however, an entirely satisfactory substitute for the administration of a direct test of communicative proficiency. First, unless the correlation between the indirect (predictor) measure and the proficiency test is perfect (a practical if not theoretical impossibility) scores on the former can never be viewed as corresponding precisely to given proficiency test scores, but must be interpreted on a probability basis. For example, using an expectancy table format, a student receiving a score of 37 on some hypothetical predictor measure might be shown to have seven chances in ten of obtaining at least a level-"N"[5] (low) rating on a certain proficiency test, four chances in ten of obtaining a level-"O" rating, and only two chances in ten of obtaining a level-"P" rating. On the basis of these results, it would be possible to conclude that the student's performance on the proficiency test, if he were to take it, would most likely fall within the "N" or possibly the "O" category, but would be quite unlikely to reach the "P" level. This information, though of some value in estimating the student's level of proficiency, is by no means so detailed and unambiguous as that which would be obtained through direct administration of the proficiency test itself.

A related disadvantage is that the statistical correspondences reported may not be accurate for students whose language background or instructional history differs appreciably from that of the original testing group, because their performance on the indirect test (especially if the test is highly specific to a given course of study or instructional method) may not "fit" their performance on the proficiency test in the same way as for the original group.

A third disadvantage, which should definitely not be overlooked, is that indirect tests of proficiency do not provide an opportunity for the student to try out his language competence in realistic communication situations. Although they may correspond in a statistical sense to direct tests of proficiency, paper-and-pencil tests, tape-recorded listening and speaking tests, and similar measures cannot have the same psychological value for the student or the same instructional impact. For this reason alone, administration of a direct test of communicative proficiency at one or more points in the student's language-learning career would be a very worthwhile undertaking.

_____

[5] These are arbitrary letters which would correspond to verbally defined levels of proficiency.

Chapter 4

Knowledge Testing

Foreign-language courses—if defined to include any teaching activities under the auspices of a school or college foreign-language staff or department—can have many different types of content and instructional goals other than or in addition to the inculcation of linguistic skills: the teaching of the "culture" of the foreign-language country is usually considered an important component of instruction from the earliest levels; advanced secondary school, college, and graduate school courses often involve the study of "literature," including an appreciation of the content, historical background, and stylistic attributes of literary works; and a number of courses intended for language majors, prospective teachers, and other "specializers" deal with what might be considered the foreign language as a subject matter, including courses in articulatory phonetics, comparative and historical linguistics, and similar areas of study in which the student learns various things about the language in much the same way that he would in studying some other body of knowledge.

Tests designed to measure student accomplishment in these three broad categories may be characterized as "knowledge" tests to indicate that they focus on determining the student's acquisition of facts or concepts rather than on measuring his linguistic competence as such. Culture, literature, and language as a subject matter may of course be taught through the medium of the foreign language, and a fairly high degree of language skill may be required for effective accomplishment in these areas, but the main teaching and testing emphasis in each case is on the conceptual message rather than the linguistic medium.

The teaching of language as a subject matter is not usually at issue in most secondary school or basic college courses, and testing procedures in this respect will not be considered here. Tests in the areas of culture and literature are of considerably more concern to the teacher at these levels, and are discussed at length below.

CULTURE TESTING

The term "culture" does not have a precise and uniform meaning within the foreign-language teaching profession. Teachers who consider that they are including "culture" as part of their instructional activities may have widely differing goals and approaches depending on their own interpretation of this term.

CULTURE AS CIVILIZATION AND FINE ARTS

To many persons, teaching the culture of the foreign-language country involves apprising students of various facts about its geography, political history, economics, governmental organizations, architecture, music and painting, famous men, and the like. Testing of the student's acquisition of this type of information is a fairly straightforward matter. Multiple-choice items can be written, each based on a particular element of knowledge. For example:

(Select the most appropriate completion for each statement.)
    The Spanish city best known for its Holy Week celebration is
      (A) Sevilla
      (B) Valladolid
      (C) Granada
      (D) Córdoba

----

*(A) Sevilla

The name Segovia is most frequently associated with the
      (A) oboe
      (B) cello
      (C) guitar
      (D) piano

----

*(C) guitar

Le Tiers-Etat des Etats-Généraux s'est constitué en Assemblée
Nationale dans
 (A) l'Orangerie du Palais du Louvre
 (B) un jeu de paume à Versailles
 (C) la cour de la Bastille démolie
 (D) le Palais du Luxembourg

----

*(B) un jeu de paume à Versailles

The first written constitution in France dates from
 (A) the reign of Charlemagne
 (B) the 13th century
 (C) the reign of Louis XVI
 (D) the Revolution of 1789

----

*(D) the Revolution of 1789

If precise diagnostic information is needed about the student's
acquisition of each item of information, a free-response format may
be employed. For example:

(Write the correct answer to each question.)
 With what French artist is the term *pointillisme* best associated?

_____

Seurat

A distinction should be made here between "hard" facts about a
country or its citizens on the one hand and matters of interpretation
or personal orientation on the other hand, which are often presented
in the guise of factual information. The following item is a typical
example:

(Select the best completion of the statement.)
 In contemporary French society, the most highly regarded per-
sons are the
 (A) industrial magnates
 (B) diplomats

    (C) religious leaders
    (D) intellectuals

----

  *(D) intellectuals

Although the teacher writing this item may feel that the French intellectuals best fit this description (and may have so informed the class), cogent arguments could be advanced in favor of each of the other answers. This item thus does not deal with a "fact" about which anyone knowledgeable in the area would concur, but rather an affirmation on the part of the test writer which might be supported by certain types of evidence and refuted by others. Test questions which deal with cultural topics often fall prey to this difficulty because there is a natural tendency on the part of the test writer to feel that his notion of the "greatest Renaissance painter," "most significant 20th-century sculptor," "turning-point battle," and so forth are universally accepted verities on the same order of certainty as geographical features and the dates of historical events. Elements of cultural information which are indeed factual are quite appropriate for testing by means of multiple-choice items or short free responses of the type shown. However, informational aspects which can be considered to some extent matters of opinion or interpretation would best be handled by means of a short essay in which the student would have the opportunity to provide evidence in support of a particular conclusion rather than simply to identify or reproduce what he considers the tester to "want" in the way of an answer.

The teaching and testing of "culture" as involving student knowledge of the foreign-language country and the accomplishments of its most notable inhabitants has a venerable history, and it is not appropriate here to discuss the general merit or pedagogical value of these activities. It should be understood, however, that this is simply one acceptation of the term "culture."

CULTURE AS PATTERNS OF LIVING

A second and quite different view of "culture" has been presented succinctly by Brooks (1968) in an important discussion of the nature and role of culture in the foreign-language classroom. Brooks identifies a number of meanings which can be given to the term "culture" and describes each using subscript numerals in the manner of a dictionary definition. The definition which Brooks analyzes at greatest length and which he identifies as of primary importance at the basic levels of instruction is his "culture₄," characterized as "the individual's role in the unending kaleidoscope of life situations of every kind and the rules and models for attitude and conduct in them. By reference to these models, every human being, from infancy onward, justifies the world to himself as best he can, associates with those around him, and relates to the social order to which he is attached" (p. 210). In more operational terms, this type of "culture" is considered to be manifested in those things which a person is expected to "think, believe, say, do, eat, wear, pay, endure, resent, honor, laugh at, fight for, and worship, in typical life situations. . . ." (p. 211).

The view of culture represented by Brooks' definition has gained the increasing attention of foreign-language teachers over the past several years and is a major topic of discussion and analysis at the present time. However, the development of appropriate teaching and testing procedures in this area still faces a number of problems, especially in the definition of instructional content and of the nature of the student mastery expected.

In regard to the content question, theoretical tools are already available to aid in this analysis. Given an accurate inventory of foreign behaviors in "typical life situations," the teacher or researcher can then compare these behaviors to those of the language learner's own culture through a process somewhat similar to contrastive linguistic analysis. Cultural patterns which have the same "form," "meaning," and "distribution"[1] in both cultures would not have to be taught formally to the language student since his own perceptions of and customary behaviors in the situations involved would correspond to those of the native inhabitants. Patterns which do not have the same behavioral features or "meanings" in the two cultures would be expected to lead to misunderstandings or mis-actions on the part of the learner: it is these patterns that would be singled out for instructional and testing purposes.

Current problems in the teaching and measurement of "culture₄" lie not so much in the theory of contrastive cultural analysis as in the actual implementation of such an analysis in a sufficiently detailed and exhaustive manner to provide a large and agreed-upon corpus of cultural points or elements to be taught in the typical school setting. At the moment, there is little consensus even on the broad categories of cultural situations or behaviors within which such an analysis might be made. Hall (1959) has listed ten basic categories

---

[1] For a definition of these terms and discussions of contrastive techniques as applied to cultural analysis, see Lado (1957, ch. 6; 1961, ch. 20).

which he considers appropriate to the objective analysis of a culture, including such aspects as "interaction," "bi-sexuality," "territoriality," "learning," and "play." Brooks, on the other hand, proposes ten other categories, including "symbolism," "value," "authority," "honor," "humor," and "spirit" (1968, p. 213). The absence of a clear consensus on the analytical categories that should be applied to cultural analysis for classroom instructional purposes makes the derivation of particular cultural points for both teaching and testing a difficult and largely individualistic matter. In the absence of close agreement on— or even general guidelines for—the types of cultural elements that should be taught and tested in the usual foreign-language course, teachers and test developers are forced to generate cultural "items" largely on the basis of their own perceptions or opinions, which might be highly atypical and in any event considerably limited in scope.

In addition to the problem of content in discussing culture of the "patterns of living" type is the question of what form the student's response should take. If the instructional goal is to modify the student's behavior in such a way that he will react in a culturally appropriate manner to a variety of real-life host-country situations, then measurement of the student's accomplishment would ideally make use of a testing arrangement in which various cultural situations could be presented "live" and in as authentic a manner as possible, and the student's behavior observed. However, technical problems involved in this "real-life situation" testing would impose considerable restraints on the number and types of cultural elements that could be presented. Situations involving bullfights, state ceremonies, sports events, and the like could certainly not be simulated with any degree of accuracy, and the content of a behaviorally-based test would instead have to be restricted to easily-presented situations such as greetings, leave-takings, appropriate use of eating utensils, and so forth.[2]

In view of the practical limitations on direct tests of culturally appropriate behavior, it would be necessary in most cases to test instead the student's *knowledge* of appropriate behavior in various cultural situations. This procedure was adopted by Seelye (1966, 1969) in developing tests of "cross-cultural awareness" to be administered to Americans living in Guatemala. Seelye's test consisted of multiple-choice items which (for the most part) presented a verbally-described situation in the item stem and various possible behaviors in or reactions to the situation in the options. The student's task was

---

[2] A few additional situations are described in Seelye (1970).

to identify the probable behavior or reactions of native Latin Americans in that situation. For example:

> A Latin American is stopped by the police and is issued a ticket.
> He would probably
> (A) argue emotionally.
> (B) say nothing.
> (C) say "I should call my lawyer."
> (D) say "Can't we settle this in another way?"

----

*(A) argue emotionally.

The relationship between the student's ability to identify culturally appropriate behavior from among several choices and the likelihood of his performing in the same way in real-life situations is not known, and would be extremely difficult to determine on an empirical basis. It could be assumed, however, that knowledge of appropriate behavior would in general have a positive correspondence with actual behavior, although the degree of such correspondence would depend on a number of factors, including especially the psychological orientation of the individual toward the foreign culture and the degree of his motivation to adapt to that culture.

"EXPLANATION" OF CULTURAL PHENOMENA

There is some question of whether the student should be asked to explain the "reasons" for particular cultural phenomena in addition to recognizing their existence. One of the distinguishing characteristics of culture of the "patterns of living" type is that members of the culture are often unable to describe or generalize about the significance or "meaning" of observed patterns. In this regard, the development of the student's ability to "explain why" particular phenomena are manifested in a culture may be considered to go beyond the attainments of the native speakers themselves. On the other hand, explanations of and generalizations about particular aspects of behavior can provide a powerful educational tool and can help to tie together a number of phenomena which the student would otherwise see only as unrelated and arbitrary.[3] Frances and Howard Nostrand (1968) identify a category of culture teaching involving an "explanation" of the observed phenomena and suggest that both

---

[3] On this point, see especially Nostrand (1966, pp. 8-9).

multiple-choice and free-response (essay) questions would be appropriate testing techniques. In the multiple-choice items which they present, a particular cultural situation is described in the stem of the item and the student is asked to select the most appropriate explanation of the situation among the answer options. For example:

A likely reason why the French shake hands more than Americans do is

    (A) they like to hold hands.

    (B) they consider it courteous to pay full attention to one person at a time.

    (C) they are effusive, demonstrative about greeting and leave-taking.

    (D) they have a superstitious fear of bad luck.

A potential drawback in the use of multiple-choice items of this type is the great difficulty of providing "distracter" options which, though clearly incorrect to the knowledgeable student, are in themselves reasonably plausible. In the preceding example, options A and D would probably not be chosen by many examinees simply because they are intrinsically quite improbable.

A related disadvantage is the necessity to greatly simplify (and possibly misrepresent) complex and detailed analyses of cultural phenomena in order to cast these into a short phrase or sentence. Free-response techniques (including both short student answers and, where indicated, longer compositions) would bypass both of the difficulties discussed, although at the expense of scoring ease. For example, the preceding multiple-choice item might be rewritten: "Explain briefly why handshaking on greeting and leave-taking is highly prevalent in France. Cite other phenomena which may be interpreted in the same way."

LITERATURE TESTING

Instruction in "literature" is a somewhat less prominent aspect of secondary-school foreign-language programs than is the teaching of "culture." Culture topics are considered an important part of the foreign-language curriculum from the beginning course onward; the teaching of "literature," on the other hand, is usually reserved for college courses or for the most advanced level of the high school program, especially the "advanced placement" courses which are intended to parallel the first college literature course in purpose and scope.[4]

READING IN THE LITERATURE COURSE

A notable characteristic of the literature course, by comparison to earlier skills courses, is that the student is asked to do a considerable amount of reading in the foreign language on his own time and without the close supervision of the teacher. It is generally assumed that students in the course are indeed reading these texts in the original language with a fairly high degree of comprehension. However, the verification of this assumption is an extremely difficult matter. A common technique to test the student's familiarity with works he has been asked to read is to pose general questions, either multiple-choice or short free-response, in which the student must demonstrate knowledge of the names and actions of characters, details of plot development, and other matters of textual content, as in the following examples:

(Select the most appropriate completion for the statement.)
Dans *Les Mouches* de Jean-Paul Sartre, quand Oreste entre en scène
    (A) Egisthe convoque le peuple d'Argos.
    (B) des femmes font des libations à une statue.
    (C) les mouches se précipitent sur lui.
    (D) Electre le rencontre mais ne le reconnaît pas.

----

  *(B) des femmes font des libations à une statue.

(Write the correct answer to the question.)
Chez qui Meursault a-t-il l'habitude de déjeuner?

_____

Céleste

Unfortunately, a high level of performance on test questions of this type cannot be considered conclusive evidence that the student has

---

[4] Lohnes (1968) discusses the contribution of the CEEB Advanced Placement program to foreign-language literature teaching at the high school level.

read with comprehension the original works. Plot summaries or native-language translations are readily available for many of the works studied in basic literature courses, and since the information necessary to answer questions on content is easily obtainable from these sources, students who make use of these aids could perform well on the test questions without ever having looked at the foreign-language text. If the test questions themselves are in the foreign language, students who have not worked with the original text may be disadvantaged to some extent through unfamiliarity with question vocabulary, but this effect would probably be slight and in no event an effective deterrent to the use of translations.

Stronger encouragement for reading the course materials in the foreign language could be provided by formally testing the comprehension of selected passages from these texts, using techniques discussed in Chapter 2. However, even tests of this type would not indicate absolutely whether students had read the works in the foreign language, since students with a high level of general reading ability would be able to understand the test passages without necessarily having read the material at an earlier time.

It seems necessary to conclude that there will always be some uncertainty in regard to the students' reading of the original foreign-language texts, and that the teacher will have to make the working assumption that his students are doing so. This assumption can be strengthened by administering formal tests of passage comprehension as part of the total testing program, by keeping the overall reading load at a reasonable level, and by admitting to the literature course only those students who are known to have developed a reasonably high level of reading proficiency through earlier course work.

Beyond the question of reading comprehension *per se,* literature courses at the secondary-school and introductory college level are usually concerned with two broad areas of instruction: the imparting of literary *information,* and the development of the student's ability to carry out various types of literary *interpretation.*

TESTING OF LITERARY INFORMATION

In the literary information area are included data on authors' lives, the existence, chronology, and content of various works, and generally agreed-on "facts" about the nature and significance of these works, especially in terms of their contribution to the overall body of literature in that language. Information of this type is usually considered necessary to acquaint the student with the broad spectrum of the foreign-language literature and to provide needed background for the informed discussion and close analysis of selected texts.

The student's acquisition of various elements of literary information can be tested through the use of multiple-choice or short free-response questions, as in the following examples:

(Select the most appropriate completion for each statement.)
Jorge Luis Borges is
(A) a Chilean playwright
(B) a Peruvian novelist
(C) a Mexican poet
(D) an Argentinian author

----

*(D) an Argentinian author

Boileau composed his *Art poétique* on the model of
(A) Plutarch
(B) Homer
(C) Horace
(D) Aristotle

----

*(C) Horace

(Write the correct answer to the question.)
In what year was Molière's *Tartuffe* first presented in its final, five-act version?

1669

The notion of the "acte gratuit" has been most thoroughly explored in the work of _____

Gide

The teaching and testing of "facts" of literary history is a quite acceptable procedure, provided it is clearly understood that the student's only responsibility in this connection—and his only learning achievement—is to retain in memory statements about authors and works which he has obtained from secondary sources rather than inferred on the basis of his own reading.

Testing of Literary Interpretation

Most teachers of literature feel that the student's learning should not be restricted to the acquisition of information but should also include the development of an ability to *interpret* literary materials. In carrying out such interpretations, the student would be expected to utilize selected elements of received information but at the same time to combine them with insights derived from his own thoughtful reading of original texts in order to produce meaningful and well-reasoned appraisals of their structure, style, intent, literary significance, and so forth. A given appraisal could involve the operations of: analysis (as in explicating the stylistic elements manifested in a given work or passage); synthesis (as in tracing correspondences in content, structure, style, theme, or purpose among various passages, works, or authors); or both.

In all cases, emphasis is placed on the student's ability to organize and present information on an active basis, and to test this ability, free-response techniques must be employed. It is theoretically possible to have the student give a spoken response in making a literary interpretation,[5] but in most cases the response is written out in the form of an "essay," "theme," "analysis," "composition," or whatever other term may be used.

In planning a composition test on literary interpretation, the teacher is faced with the basic and very important question of the *language* in which the students will be asked to write. Many teachers feel that there is only one valid answer: since the literature course is after all a course within the foreign-language curriculum, the students should be expected to use the foreign language. Such a procedure is considered desirable not only to maintain pedagogical consistency across courses but also to provide a further opportunity for the student to practice his writing skills.

On the other hand, certain disadvantages to the use of the foreign language can be identified. A basic problem is that of confounding the measurement of students' literary interpretation ability with skill in writing the foreign language. Students who have some difficulty in writing the language in an accurate and fluent manner may be con-

---

[5] This is indeed occasionally the case in graduate school "oral" examinations for literature majors.

siderably hindered in responding to a particular interpretation topic, even though they would be able to carry out an excellent discussion of the topic in their native language. At the other extreme, students who have a very good command of the written language may produce compositions which are somewhat lacking in strict content terms but which are linguistically quite impressive. In these cases, the teacher may be overly influenced by the form of the student's response and assign it a higher score than would be justified by its informational content.

Further, it may be wondered whether the type of writing involved in literary interpretation is of particular utility to the student in developing his writing skills for other practical uses. The terminology of literary comparison and analysis is largely unique to its field, and unless the student is planning to do advanced work in literature much of the lexicon needed to write on such topics in the foreign language will be of little further value outside of the course itself.

The composition topics presented in a given test will of course depend on the works read by the students, instructional emphases, and other factors unique to the course situation. However, there are certain general criteria which such topics should meet regardless of their exact content. First, it would be important for the topic to present a novel interpretation situation. As part of the regular class work, the teacher will probably have led the class through various interpretation exercises, perhaps discussing in detail the overall structure, imagery, and author's intent in a particular work. A test topic which asked the student to "discuss the structure, imagery, and author's intent" of the class-discussed work would constitute a simple exercise in recall and would not require the student to demonstrate developed interpretive skills. On the other hand, a similar question posed of a work which had *not* been discussed in class would constitute a valid test of this ability.

The composition topic should also be very clearly stated and closely delimited. Broad and vaguely expressed composition topics such as those requesting the student to "discuss the literary importance" of a certain author or work are much too general to be treated adequately in the test situation. In addition, students tend to take highly varied approaches to such "open-ended" topics and to produce compositions which vary so widely in content as to make uniform scoring extremely difficult.

Teachers should realize that only a quite limited number of aspects can be discussed by the student within the testing period, and should thus specify in the topic itself those relatively few areas in which the student should concentrate his attention. The following examples are drawn from previously administered *CEEB Advanced Placement* examinations in French, and show topics which are each intended to be answered within a one-hour period.

° Dans *Le Tartuffe* (ou dans *Le Misanthrope*), discutez le comique par rapport 1) à l'intrigue, 2) au caractère, 3) au langage.

° Quelles sont les institutions politiques, sociales et religieuses de son temps auxquelles Rabelais s'attaque dans son *Pantagruel?* Montrez les différents moyens littéraires par lesquels il les combat en donnant des exemples.

° Le thème de l'évasion chez Baudelaire, c'est-à-dire: le départ, l'exotisme, le désir d'échapper à la laideur de la vie. Citez quelques poèmes dans lesquels ce thème est exprimé et discutez avec précision les techniques poétiques (symboles, images, métaphores, etc.) utilisées par Baudelaire.

Procedures used to score the student compositions will vary depending on whether the compositions are written in the foreign language or in the native language. If the native language is used, the composition will of course be evaluated only for its informational content from a "literature-interpretation" viewpoint. If the foreign language is used, the teacher has the choice of scoring only the content aspects of the composition or of evaluating also the linguistic quality of the student's writing.

If only the informational content is to be scored, the teacher should make every effort not to be influenced by missing accents, misspellings, absent or inappropriate grammatical agreements, and so forth, and to look only for comprehensibly expressed items of information. However, in no event should the students be informed that writing accuracy will not be counted in scoring: to do so may tempt students to write rapidly and carelessly, and as a result the test would constitute "writing practice" of a sort quite opposite to that intended by the teacher.

If both content and writing quality are to be considered, it must be decided whether both aspects will be combined in a single global appreciation of the student's performance or whether each will be scored separately. Global ratings could be assigned more quickly than separate ratings, but they would be very difficult to interpret, since a given student's score would reflect unknown proportions of "content quality" and "writing quality."

Separate ratings for content and writing quality can be carried out in a number of ways. The teacher could read a student's composition and make ratings of both aspects immediately after the single reading. A major drawback to this procedure is that it requires the teacher constantly to alter his "mental set" between content and writing quality and to risk blurring the distinction between the two in assigning scores. A preferable technique is to carry out the scoring in two separate stages. In the first stage, the teacher reads and evaluates each composition from a content point of view and ignores linguistic aspects to the greatest extent possible. After all of the papers have been read for content, the teacher re-reads each composition in terms of the linguistic quality of the student's writing. Alternatively, two teachers can score the tests in concert, one evaluating only content and the other only the writing aspect.

The standards to be followed in scoring both content and writing should be clearly outlined before the papers are read. If the topic has been carefully prepared, it will in itself imply certain content elements which the student's response should incorporate. The teacher could allocate a certain proportion of the total points for the composition to each of these elements; within each, higher or lower scores could be assigned depending on the adequacy of the student's handling of that particular element. A separate content scoring outline would probably have to be developed for each new test, since the number of elements at issue in the topic would probably vary, and the detailed attributes of an ideal response to each element would also change.

Scoring procedures for evaluating the written quality of the student's composition could be more generally expressed, and could be utilized in more than one test situation. Various linguistic categories can be identified (e.g., vocabulary, grammatical accuracy) and a three- to five-point scale of quality adopted for each category. This scoring technique has been discussed in detail in Chapter 2. If desired, "content" and "writing" scores could be combined into a single total test score, but the two sub-scores should also be reported to the student as additional diagnostic information.

Chapter 5
The Role of Published Tests

In the preceding chapters, foreign-language tests have been classified and discussed according to the measurement purposes which they are intended to serve. It will be useful at this point to categorize testing instruments on the basis of the persons or organizations involved in their production. In addition to *locally-prepared tests* developed by a teacher, school, or school system (and discussed in detail in Chapter 2) are three other categories of tests which are developed and published by agencies external to the classroom teacher or school system. These are: *textbook-related tests, secure standardized tests,* and *generally-available standardized tests.*

"Textbook-related" tests are instruments provided by the publisher of a foreign-language textbook, textbook series, or other instructional program, and designed for use with a particular set of instructional materials.

"Standardized" tests, both "secure" and "generally-available," are not based on a single course of study but are instead intended to be appropriate for students who have had a certain amount of language instruction without reference to the specific teaching program. The term "standardized" refers to the fact that the tests are designed for administration in a carefully planned and clearly outlined manner which permits students taking the test to encounter highly comparable testing conditions regardless of the time or location at which they take the test. Standardized tests are also in most cases *norm referenced;* this means that summary information on the performance of one or more groups of students who have taken the test previously is presented—usually in the form of percentile equivalents—to aid the test user in interpreting the scores of his own students.

"Secure" standardized tests are those used in large-scale testing programs administered on a nation-wide, or in some cases international basis under carefully controlled conditions and typically only on certain specified testing dates. Test booklets and related materials in secure programs are not in general available for examination by persons other than the students taking the test, and test scoring is usually carried out centrally by the organization conducting the testing program.

"Generally-available" standardized tests are for the most part similar to secure standardized tests, except that they are sold or loaned to teachers or other legitimate educational users for administration and scoring under local auspices and for locally-defined purposes. Even though the publisher of a "generally-available" test does not have direct control on administration conditions, detailed descriptions of the procedures to be followed are provided the test user and he is urged to follow these procedures as closely as possible in order to maintain the standardized quality of the tests.

Each of these three types of published tests is discussed in the following sections.

TEXTBOOK-RELATED TESTS

A great number of foreign-language textbook programs provide series of tests to be used with their teaching materials. It is not appropriate here to compare the test offerings of different textbook publishers, but it is possible to make the general observation that these tests vary widely in quality and must be carefully scrutinized by the prospective user. Some textbook-related tests are little more than neatly printed blackboard quizzes typical of those which would be produced by a teacher unfamiliar with many of the basic principles of foreign-language testing; others are quite sophisticated instruments which include tape-recorded listening comprehension and speaking measures as well as reading and writing tests. The teacher who is considering the use of a textbook-related test series would be well advised to review these instruments very closely along the lines previously discussed before making a decision on their use. The mere fact that these tests have been published should not be taken as indicative of their quality; this matter must be determined in each individual case.

TEXTBOOK-RELATED TESTS AND LOCALLY-DEVELOPED TESTS

By virtue of the position which they occupy within the instructional system, textbook-related tests have enormous potential as valid and effective measures of classroom achievement. Because their prospective audience is as wide as the total number of schools in which the textbook materials are used, a series of well-formulated textbook-related tests can provide achievement information for a much greater number of students than can similar tests produced by individual teachers or local groups.

A comparison of the total manpower involved in developing local tests for each classroom or school system, in contrast to that needed to produce a single, widely-published set of textbook-related materials, must favor the latter. To the extent that the classroom teacher follows the textbook program in a reasonably close and consistent manner, properly developed textbook-related tests would provide the same kinds of achievement information (both diagnostic and general) that could be obtained through the use of teacher-made tests, and with a considerable economy of time and effort at the local level.

This is not by any means intended to imply that teacher-made tests could be abandoned or that a thorough grounding in the theory and technique of foreign-language testing would not continue to be an important component of the teacher's professional background and abilities. Indeed, for the frequent occasions in which the teacher intentionally departs from certain portions of the textbook lessons or presents "enrichment" materials not part of the regular program, locally-prepared tests would be needed to complement the published textbook tests. In addition, sophistication in testing principles and techniques would be needed in order for the teacher to interpret properly the information provided by the textbook tests and to discern the strengths and weaknesses of the published instruments.

The testing techniques, item formats, and interpretive rules governing textbook-based tests are essentially identical to those previously discussed for locally-prepared achievement tests. Textbook tests (again, assuming a high-quality product) are considered to have some superiority over locally-developed tests not because of any inherent advantages from a measurement point of view but because they represent a more efficient use of test development time and manpower when considered on an overall "systems" basis.

TEXTBOOK-RELATED TESTS AND STANDARDIZED TESTS

On the other hand, textbook-related tests are both operationally and conceptually preferable to standardized tests for the measurement of classroom achievement, especially in its more diagnostic aspects. A major advantage is that developers of textbook-related tests have available in the course syllabus a highly detailed description both of the specific morphological and structural elements introduced in the course and of their chronological sequencing. Thus, in preparing a test to be administered at a given point in the course, the test writers can avoid the problem of introducing novel material which, by definition, is not a valid object of classroom achievement testing.

By contrast, developers of standardized tests cannot follow a specific textbook syllabus but must base test content on those elements which students following a generalized, "typical" course would be expected to have encountered at a given level of instruction. Although there may be in many cases a high congruence between the classroom experiences of a given group of students and the content of a generally-available standardized test, there will usually be a certain number of syntactical or morphological elements included in the test which the students in the course will not have encountered or to which they will have been exposed only peripherally. Thus, the teacher using a standardized test for achievement measurement purposes must carefully review the test materials to assure himself that there is a usefully close correspondence between test content and the content of the course up to the time of testing.

A similar problem may be seen in the area of test lexicon. Although detailed experimental studies have not been carried out in this regard, it is generally considered that the student's performance on standardized foreign-language achievement tests depends to a certain, and perhaps substantial, extent on his familiarity with the test vocabulary, in the sense that if he does not know the meaning of certain words appearing in the test items, he may be hindered in answering these items, even though he has the requisite command of the morphological and syntactical elements involved.

If the words in question are those which the student "should know" (i.e., are those previously covered in the course), his failure to answer the item may be a legitimate reflection of his lack of "achievement" in the course.[1] However, if the student has never had the opportunity to encounter certain words—as might be true of the lexicon appearing in a generally oriented standardized test—he may be unfairly penalized in his response to the test items. In his discussion of the well-known "Pennsylvania study," Carroll (1969) suggested that students following particular textbook programs may have been differentially advantaged or penalized in their performance on the project tests through greater or lesser familiarity with the test vocabulary. In reviewing the same project, Valette (1969) made detailed comparisons of the vocabulary used in the project's reading, listening comprehension, and writing tests against the lexical content of selected textbook programs, and found that there were substantial differences in the amount of test vocabulary included in these programs. On the strength of these comparisons it was suggested that at least some of the observed differences in test scores of groups using different textbook programs could be attributed to differing degrees of familiarity with the test vocabulary.

It is difficult to make a firm statement that a novel lexical item appearing in a test passage or item will necessarily have a disruptive effect on the student's performance. Depending on the item format and linguistic context involved in a particular testing situation, a given item of vocabulary might merely serve as "window dressing" having no bearing on the student's response or might constitute a critical element with which the student would have to be familiar in order to answer the question properly. In any event, undesirable measurement effects attributable to the presence of previously "untaught" vocabulary should be taken into account in evaluating the usefulness of a given standardized test as a measure of classroom language achievement in a particular course setting.

A further advantage of textbook-related tests over standardized tests as measures of classroom achievement is the greater latitude which they offer for using free-response formats. Since standardized foreign-language tests are designed with large-scale testing applications in mind, every effort is made to simplify and facilitate the administration and scoring process. Free-response formats are adopted only for speaking and writing tests (which require this approach for

---

[1] This of course refers only to tests of general achievement, since diagnostic tests aimed at measuring accuracy of pronunciation, control of syntax, or other non-lexical aspects of the student's performance may be adversely affected by the presence of vocabulary elements with which the student is not familiar.

valid measurement) and multiple-choice techniques are used to test the two passive skills of listening comprehension and reading.[2]

As discussed in Chapter 2, there are numerous diagnostic achievement testing situations within the listening comprehension and reading areas in which a free-response format would be suitable and indeed preferred over a multiple-choice format. Low-volume, teacher-scored textbook tests share with locally-prepared tests the possibility of easily and routinely incorporating free-response procedures wherever they are considered appropriate to the measurement purpose; this flexibility is not, however, readily available in the standardized testing context.

SECURE STANDARDIZED TESTS

The contact of the foreign-language teacher or supervisor with secure standardized tests will probably be limited to taking one or more of these tests in the course of his academic or teaching career, or to having his students take them at various "decision points" in their instructional history.

Although a few secure foreign-language tests are offered under other auspices, the great majority are developed by and administered under the supervision of Educational Testing Service (ETS), either in one of its own programs—such as the National Teacher Examinations—or on behalf of sponsoring organizations such as the College Entrance Examination Board (CEEB) or the Graduate Record Examinations Board (GREB).

Most of the secure testing programs administered by ETS are not devoted exclusively to foreign-language testing but, instead, offer foreign-language tests as one of several different subject matter areas. For example, the *CEEB Achievement Test* program includes examinations in American History and Social Studies, Biology, Chemistry, English Composition, Mathematics, and several other academic areas in addition to foreign languages.

General Characteristics

The fact that the foreign-language tests must share common format, test timing, and administration procedures with other subject-

---

[2] There is no theoretical barrier to the use of free-response techniques in standardized listening comprehension or reading tests; the observation made here is simply that test developers have, for the sake of testing efficiency and practicality, consistently used multiple-choice format in measuring these two skills.

matter tests, together with the very large testing volumes involved, places certain restrictions on the measurement procedures employed, the chief of which is that multiple-choice format must be used throughout. A significant exception is the somewhat lower-volume *CEEB Advanced Placement* program, which uses free-response procedures in certain sections of its examinations.

Another characteristic of most of the secure testing programs is that they make use of several alternate forms of a given test. These different forms are cycled in rather complex sequences among the various administration dates. Test offerings are regularly updated by the inclusion of new forms of the test and the retirement of earlier forms. This procedure helps to maintain test security and, in addition, permits the gradual modification of testing procedures and content to reflect changing curricular emphases.

In order to eliminate measurement differences across candidates attributable to the fact that different test forms are being used, a procedure known as *score equating* is carried out. Typically, this involves including in each new test form a certain number of questions from an earlier form of the test. Student performance on these questions is statistically compared to the performance of previous groups of students on the same questions to establish an adjustment formula whereby any slight difference in the overall difficulty level of the new test by comparison to earlier tests can be taken into account in the scoring process. The end product of the equating procedure is a *scaled score* utilizable as "common currency" in comparing the performance level of different students regardless of the time at which they took the test and the particular test form involved.

OVERVIEW OF SECURE TESTING PROGRAMS

A brief description of the various secure foreign-language testing programs administered by ETS will point up both the nature and the scope of "secure" standardized testing in the foreign-language field.

CEEB ACHIEVEMENT TESTS

Primary Testing Purpose: Selection of secondary-school applicants for college study (in conjunction with *CEEB Scholastic Aptitude Tests.*)

Languages: French, German, Hebrew, Italian, Russian, Spanish.

Description of Tests: Two types of tests are now offered in the Achievement program, depending on the language and the administration date. Listening-reading tests, containing a 20-minute listening comprehension section and a 40-minute reading section, are offered in French, German, Italian, Russian, and Spanish. Sixty-minute reading-only tests are also offered in these five languages and in modern Hebrew. For the listening-reading tests, sub-scores for each skill section are provided as well as a total test score.[3]

CEEB ADVANCED PLACEMENT TESTS

Primary Testing Purpose: Identification of high-school students meriting advanced course placement or course exemption in college.

Languages: French, German, Spanish.

Description of Tests: Advanced Placement Examinations are three hours in length and serve as "final examinations" for a prescribed course of college caliber taught in participating secondary schools. Both multiple-choice and free-response (essay) formats are used. In addition to the literature-oriented course and examination offered in French, German, and Spanish, a French-language program was introduced in 1970-71. The language course parallels a college-level "composition and conversation" course, and the related examination comprises direct tests of all four language-skill areas. The listening comprehension and reading sections use multiple-choice format, while the speaking and writing tests require the student to tape-record his responses or to write them out in the test booklet. The free-response sections of the Advanced Placement examinations are scored by a trained group of secondary-school and college teachers who meet annually for this purpose.

GRADUATE RECORD EXAMINATIONS—ADVANCED TESTS

Primary Testing Purpose: Selection of college students for graduate school study (in conjunction with *GRE Aptitude Tests*).

Languages: French, German, Spanish.

Description of Tests: Three-hour tests covering reading comprehension, literary knowledge and interpretation, literary and political history, and various cultural topics.

GRADUATE SCHOOL FOREIGN LANGUAGE TESTS

Primary Testing Purpose: Measurement of the student's proficiency

---

[3] The listening-reading tests, administered for the first time in May 1971, constitute a real "breakthrough" in language testing within the framework of the CEEB Achievement test program. Administration of a listening comprehension section at the many hundreds of testing centers involved required extensive changes in administration arrangements, data-processing procedures, and other operational aspects of the testing program. Interesting accounts of earlier CEEB efforts to develop and make available tape-recorded listening tests on a supplementary basis may be found in Dyer (1954) and Scheider (1962).

in reading professional literature in a field of graduate specialization.

Languages: French, German, Russian, Spanish.

Description of Tests: Two-hour test. Includes common sections testing basic reading vocabulary and structure, and alternate sections testing general reading comprehension of material appropriate to the natural sciences, social sciences, and humanities (candidate selects section most appropriate to his area of specialization).[4]

NATIONAL TEACHER EXAMINATIONS

Primary Testing Purpose: To provide information useful in the selection and evaluation of teaching personnel. (The Common Examinations in this program are devoted to the measurement of general education and professional education background; the Teaching Area Examinations measure competence and professional background in specific subject matter areas.)

Languages: French, German, Spanish.

Description of Tests: These two-hour tests contain separate sections on listening comprehension and reading, language analysis (phonetics, morphology, and syntax of the target language), and "cultural backgrounds" (questions on the civilization and culture of the target language country).

GENERALLY-AVAILABLE STANDARDIZED TESTS

Standardized foreign-language tests which are available for administration by the classroom teacher or other school personnel offer the measurement advantages characteristic of standardized tests (straightforward and well-planned administration procedures; possibility of comparing student scores to those of large-scale norming groups), and are free of the test-availability and administration date restrictions of tests in secure programs.

OVERVIEW OF RECENTLY-DEVELOPED TESTS

The period extending roughly from 1960-67 may be considered the "golden age" of generally-available standardized test development in the foreign-language field. Under contracts from the U.S. Office of Education, and using NDEA funds, two major standardized test

---

[4] Clark (1968) provides a more extensive description of the GSFLT program and summarizes the results of a related questionnaire survey of graduate school foreign-language testing practices.

batteries were developed through the collaborative efforts of the Modern Language Association of America and Educational Testing Service. The first of these, the *MLA Foreign Language Proficiency Tests for Teachers and Advanced Students,* consisted of separate skills tests (listening comprehension, reading comprehension, speaking, and writing), each in two parallel forms, for five different languages: French, German, Italian, Russian, and Spanish.[5] In addition to the skills tests, separate tests were developed in each language covering the areas of Applied Linguistics and Civilization and Culture. A Professional Preparation test, common to all languages and including such topics as general professional information and language teaching methodology, was also prepared.

As indicated by the official title of the battery, the tests were designed for administration to teachers and teacher candidates in the various languages and also to students at the higher levels of proficiency (e.g., college or graduate-school students specializing in the language). A major use of the new tests (informally referred to as the "MLA teacher tests" or "MLA advanced proficiency tests") was in the pre- and post-testing of participants in the NDEA summer language institutes. A number of colleges and universities, state departments of education, and other agencies have also used these tests for student selection or placement, teacher certification, and similar purposes.[6]

A second, lower-level series of skill tests in French, German, Italian, Russian, and Spanish was developed under MLA-ETS auspices and with U.S. Office of Education funding between 1960-1963. The *MLA-Cooperative Foreign Language Tests* consist of separate tests of listening comprehension, speaking, reading, and writing, each in alternate forms and at two ability levels. The "L"-level tests are intended for students in the first or second year of high-school language study or the first or second semester of college study; the "M" level tests

---

[5] These tests, initially administered on a secure basis under ETS auspices, have recently been released for general use by schools, universities, and other authorized agencies. They are available through the Cooperative Tests and Services division of ETS as the *MLA-Cooperative Foreign Language Proficiency Tests.* (N.B.—This battery should not be confused with the lower-level *MLA-Cooperative Foreign Language Tests,* distributed through the same source. To avoid this possibility, the original title of the MLA advanced proficiency tests has been retained in the present paragraphs.)

[6] Starr (1962) describes the development and early use of the MLA advanced proficiency battery.

are appropriate for students in third- or fourth-year high-school courses or third- or fourth-semester college courses.[7]

An additional battery of skills tests for use at the high-school or early college level was developed by Pimsleur and published by Harcourt, Brace and World in 1967. The *Pimsleur Modern Foreign Language Proficiency Tests*, in French, Spanish, and German versions, are available at two levels, designated Form A and Form C. Form A is intended for use with junior or senior high-school students completing a "first level" course and Form C, for students completing a "second level" course. These two forms are also considered appropriate for college students completing one or two semesters of language study, respectively.[8]

All three test batteries use essentially similar testing formats in a given skill area. The listening comprehension tests are based on spoken stimuli delivered by a tape recording which also gives the test directions and times the pauses for student response. All test questions are printed multiple-choice items in the foreign language. The reading comprehension tests are also in multiple-choice format; test passages and answer options are printed in the foreign language in the student's booklet.

In the speaking tests, stimuli are presented both in the test booklet (e.g., through pictures to be described, printed passages to be read aloud) and by a test tape (e.g., phrases to be imitated as closely as possible, spoken questions to be answered orally). The student must record all of his responses on a separate "student response tape" for later evaluation by the teacher or other rater. The writing tests require the student to write in his test booklet single words, sentences, or longer compositions in response to various printed stimuli. Like the speaking tests, the writing tests must be scored by the teacher or other qualified person.[9]

Test Development Procedures

In order to characterize the nature and role of standardized lan-

---

[7] For a more detailed description of the *MLA-Cooperative Foreign Language Tests*, see Bryan (1966) and Clark (1965) (review).

[8] The Pimsleur tests have been reviewed by Hakstian *et al.* (1969).

[9] In addition to the "four skills" batteries described above, a number of standardized tests in individual skill areas are available for local use. These include the *Common Concepts Foreign Language Tests*—a listening comprehension test published by the California Test Bureau—and the *CEEB Placement Tests* (separate listening comprehension and reading tests) available through ETS. The *Placement Tests* are recently retired forms of the *CEEB Achievement Tests;* their use is restricted to placement and counseling at the college level.

guage tests more fully, it will be useful to describe in some detail the procedures typically followed in developing, administering on a trial basis, and establishing normative data for a standardized language test. The process described below was followed by MLA/ETS in developing the MLA advanced proficiency tests and the MLA-Cooperative tests, and is typical, with some variations in detail, of the development of tests in secure programs as well.

Early in the test development process, a group of persons competent in the test language (usually teachers of the language at the level for which the test is intended) meet with testing specialists as a test development committee. One of the first tasks of the committee is to develop specifications for the overall content of the test. Generally speaking, these content specifications do not identify the specific linguistic elements to be included in particular test items but, rather, delineate somewhat broader categories which should be represented in the test.

For example, a reading comprehension test or test section might be planned to include a certain number of discrete items testing the student's familiarity with lexicon which most students at that level would be expected to have encountered. Other sections of the test might present longer texts drawn or revised from certain specified types of written passages: expository prose, dramatic materials, poetry, and the like. The proportion of the test to be devoted to each type of material is usually established at this time, and the item types to be used are also discussed and agreed upon.

On the basis of these general specifications, committee members each prepare a certain number of draft items. More items than will be needed in the final test are written in order to allow for the inevitable attrition that takes place during the item review process. After the draft items of all committee members have been assembled, they are distributed to the other members of the committee for review. Suggested changes are outlined through correspondence, and the test items are formally accepted, revised, or rejected at a second meeting of the committee. Items which the committee considers fully acceptable are approved for pretesting, the next step in the development process.

The pretesting of potential test items and the examination of the resulting information offers a very powerful means of further checking and refining test materials before they are administered operationally. To carry out this activity, one or more pretests are developed which incorporate the draft items in the form approved by the committee on the basis of its first review. The pretests are designed to parallel the operational form of the test as closely as possible in the total number of items, sequencing of test sections, administration instructions, total time allotment, and so forth. These pretests are administered to groups of students closely similar in age, grade level, and language study background to those students who will be taking the test in its final version.

Data from the pretest administrations are processed statistically in the form of *item analyses* which give detailed information about the performance of each of the test items. Although the item analysis techniques used in a particular situation may vary in detail, three basic types of information are usually obtained: 1) a measure of the overall *difficulty* of the item for the group tested, 2) an index of the item's *reliability,* and 3) information on the *performance of the item options.*

A common measure of item difficulty is simply the proportion of students who answer the item correctly. For example, an item answered successfully by 72 percent of the students is considered a much easier item than one answered correctly by only 35 percent of the students. In developing the final form of the test, a certain number of easy, moderately difficult, and quite difficult items are included, in proportions which depend on the purpose of the test and the overall level of difficulty sought.

Item reliability is usually determined using the statistic known as the *biserial correlation* or "r-biserial." This statistic relates student performance on individual test items to some more general criterion, usually scores on the test as a whole. If those students who obtain a high total score on the test tend to answer the item correctly (and conversely, if those students who obtain a low total score on the test tend to answer it incorrectly), the biserial correlation will be relatively high. If, on the other hand, students who perform well on the test as a whole tend to answer the item incorrectly (and vice versa), the biserial correlation will have a lower value.

Pretested items with low "r-biserials" are reviewed carefully for possible flaws. For example, one of the distracter options prepared by the item writer might be so sophisticated (even though factually incorrect) that it would mislead even the better students into choosing it in preference to the correct answer.

These and other problems suggested by a low biserial correlation may also be revealed through close analysis of answer option data. Various statistical procedures may be used in this regard: one of the simplest is to tabulate the number (or percentage) of students selecting each answer option and to calculate the average total test score of each of these groups. It would be expected that the group choosing the correct answer would have the highest average test score and that students having lower total scores would tend to select one of the incorrect alternatives. The number of students choosing each of the "distracter" options can also be indicative of item performance: if only a small percentage of the total student group selects a particular option, this tends to indicate that the option is not "appealing" even to the less qualified students and as a result is failing to contribute effectively to the working of the test item.[10]

Each pretest item is carefully reviewed on the basis of the item analysis data. Items which meet high linguistic standards, which are at a suitable level of difficulty, and which have satisfactory reliability and selection-of-options characteristics are approved as candidates for inclusion in the final form of the test. Items requiring extensive revision are either discarded or revised and re-pretested to check on the success of the revision.

The final selection of items to appear in the operational form of the test takes into account a number of interrelated factors including the difficulty level of the individual item, the reliability of the item, and its specific linguistic content. In some cases, an item having somewhat lower (although satisfactory) reliability may be selected because it reflects important linguistic content or is at a certain level of difficulty which should be represented in the test.

Once the final form of the test is printed and any additional test materials produced (such as listening comprehension test tapes or records), large-scale administrations are conducted in order to establish test norms and to obtain related statistical information.

DEVELOPMENT AND USE OF NORMS

The concept of norming may be easily explained. This is a procedure whereby test score information obtained in prior test administrations to selected student groups is presented as a benchmark against which the test scores of "local" students or student groups can be contrasted and interpreted. For example, the test developers might identify a "norming sample" of several hundred second-year

---

[10] The item analysis information described is not restricted to standardized tests but can also be obtained for locally-prepared tests provided that necessary data-processing facilities are available. Diederich (1964) describes a simplified item analysis procedure for locally-prepared tests that can be carried out in the classroom and in which the students themselves participate.

high-school language students. The new test would be administered
to the students in this sample and the score data obtained would
be presented in a *table of norms* appearing in the test manual or
separate publication.

Normative data are usually shown in the form of *percentile ranks*
corresponding to the different score levels for the test in question.
For example, a norms table might show that a test score of 37 corresponds to the "95th percentile." This means that of all the students
in the norming group, 95 percent of them obtained a test score lower
than 37. An equivalent statement would be that if some "new"
student were to take the test and obtain a score of 37, this would
indicate that his score on the test was higher than that of 95 percent
of the students in the original norming sample.

A note of caution is required at this point. The observed score
of the student (and also, the observed scores of the members of the
norming sample) is subject to the measurement fluctuations discussed
earlier in connection with the standard error of test scores. A single
student score is thus not a precise indication of the student's ability
level but rather an estimate of the average score that he would obtain
if he were to take the same test or a similar test on a number of
different occasions. Percentile scores (or other types of normative
information) must accordingly be interpreted so as to take this
inevitab!e variation into account.

In order to facilitate the proper interpretation of test scores, some
publishers report normative information in the form of *percentile
bands* in addition to the percentile ranks. For example, a test score
of 37 might be shown as falling within a percentile band of 93 to
98. Test scores which fall within the same percentile band are not
usually considered to differ significantly, or in other words, the imprecision of the test scores is such that the only warranted statement
about the student's level of performance would be that it can be
considered to fall within the 93rd-to-98th percentile range.[11]

The accuracy and usefulness of a particular set of norms depend
among other things on the number of students included in the norming sample. A rule of thumb is that a minimum of 200 test scores is
required to provide reasonably stable data; additional scores are of
course desirable, and in some cases several thousand students may be
included in a norming sample.

---

[11] For examples of percentile bands and further discussion of their use,
see the Booklet of Norms and the Handbook accompanying the *MLA-
Cooperative Foreign Language Tests*.

The use of a large number of students is by no means a sufficient condition for valid and useful norms: of crucial importance is the manner in which the norming sample is selected. As previously outlined, the basic purpose of test norming is to make it possible to compare student scores against the performance of a group of students who have certain specified charactertistics. Unless the norming study is carefully conceived and properly carried out, there is a strong possibility that the resulting norms will not be representative of any clearly defined student group and, as such, will fail to have a clear and useful "meaning" for score comparison purposes. If, for example, the test developer intends to construct general norms for "second-year high-school language students" but draws his norming sample exclusively from students in the immediate geographical area, the norms may be seriously biased because students in the area might be appreciably different in their level of language learning from that of a broader and more generalized group of second-year students drawn from many different classes, geographical areas, and school systems. Care in the original design of the norming sample and diligence in carrying out the sampling plan will minimize problems of this nature, and it is also the responsibility of the test developer to describe the organization and operation of his norming program in sufficient detail for the prospective test user to appraise its adequacy.

Test publishers cannot, of course, provide norms based on all possible student groups in which the test user might be interested, but must limit their norming activities to rather broadly defined student groups. For example, the *Pimsleur French Proficiency Tests* are accompanied by two tables of norms, one based on the scores of 4,543 "first-level" students in junior and senior high schools (combined), and one based on the scores of 3,052 "second-level" students. The *MLA-Cooperative Tests* offer somewhat more extensive—though still quite general—norms, including for many language/level combinations separate norms for "traditional" and "audiolingual" classes.

Although published norms provide the teacher or other test user very worthwhile information on how "local" student performance compares with that of a broad cross-section of students at the same general level of instruction, more detailed comparisons are often needed for a particular measurement purpose. For example, it may be desirable to develop norms based on the performance of students within a given school system, or norms for students participating in a special "summer-abroad" program. It is a relatively easy matter to develop the necessary norms at the local level (by comparison to other statistical activities such as carrying out a validity study for a placement testing program, or making detailed item analyses of locally-developed tests). A four-page brochure entitled "Constructing and Using Local Norms" is available from the Cooperative Tests and Services office at ETS; textbooks on educational measurement also describe norming procedures in detail.

MEASUREMENT USES OF STANDARDIZED TESTS

It will be useful in summary to review the usefulness of generally-available standardized tests with respect to the various measurement purposes identified in previous chapters. With few exceptions, standardized tests offer little measurement information of a highly diagnostic sort. Listening comprehension and reading tests—as a result of both the multiple-choice format employed and the fact that the bulk of the test items do not focus on a particular aspect of syntax, morphology, or lexicon—cannot in general provide useful feedback on the student's acquisition of discrete linguistic elements. In certain sections of typical speaking and writing tests, the student is asked to carry out somewhat more precisely defined activities. For example, in the first section of the MLA advanced proficiency speaking tests, the student is asked to imitate short phrases containing one or two "critical sounds" which are scored as correct or incorrect. In one part of the MLA-Cooperative Writing tests, the student fills in incomplete sentences with a single specified word or rewrites short sentences, changing person, number, or gender in a predetermined manner. However, substantial proportions of the speaking and writing tests in both batteries are devoted to more generally oriented exercises (e.g., extended discourse, writing of compositions), and the teacher thus faces the very practical question of whether it is worthwhile to administer the entire test purely for the sake of the diagnostic information available in certain sub-sections. Furthermore, the linguistic elements tested in these sub-sections may not include the particular items of information in which the teacher is primarily interested.

As measures of general achievement in the foreign language, standardized tests (in all four skill areas) may be of value provided that the test content—as determined through close examination of the test materials—does not depart appreciably from that of the course in which its use is contemplated. This factor is likely to be of most significance at the early levels of instruction, in which both the structures and the lexicon to which the student has been exposed are more limited than at the higher levels and more particular to the specific instructional materials involved.

Current standardized tests are not at all closely akin to the performance-oriented proficiency tests described in Chapter 3, and as such would be of questionable validity as direct measures of communicative competence. Standardized skills tests may be of some utility as indirect measures of communicative proficiency, but the necessary correlational studies are largely lacking at the present time.

The MLA advanced proficiency battery contains a "civilization and culture" test which the teacher may find useful as a measure of the student's knowledge in these areas. Close examination of the test questions asked would be needed to determine whether the material included is considered appropriate for the students tested. Since there is a virtually unlimited number of possible "facts" about the history, fine arts, etc. of the target-language country, the particular items included in the published test may not correspond in any useful degree to the specific topics covered in the course.

Probably the most useful application of standardized language tests—in addition to the normative information which they provide—is in connection with course placement, especially the placement of students with differing language study backgrounds and for which a generalized measure of achievement is required. Since these tests are "ready-made" and are accompanied by detailed administration instructions, their use would be particularly welcomed by the busy teacher or supervisor charged with the responsibility of rapidly allocating to classes large numbers of incoming students. In this regard, it is somewhat unfortunate that writing and speaking tests in the standardized batteries require specialized and expensive scoring procedures and as a result have not been widely utilized for placement or other measurement purposes by the foreign-language teaching profession. It may be hoped that continued developmental research, including the application of increasingly more sophisticated technological aids, will at some future date make the frequent and effective use of active skills tests a practical reality in the majority of school settings.

References

Abercrombie, David. "Conversation and Spoken Prose," *English Language Teaching*, Vol. XVIII, no. 1 (1963), pp. 10-16.

Agard, Frederick B. and Robert J. Di Pietro. *The Sounds of English and Italian.* (Chicago: The University of Chicago Press, 1965).

Asher, James J. "The Total Physical Response Approach to Second Language Learning," *Modern Language Journal*, Vol. LIII, no. 1 (Jan. 1969), pp. 3-17.

Brière, Eugène J. "Are We Really Measuring Proficiency with our Foreign Language Tests?," *Foreign Language Annals*, Vol. 4, no. 4 (May 1971), pp. 385-391.

Brooks, Nelson. *Language Learning: Theory and Practice*, second edition (New York: Harcourt, Brace and World, 1964).

———. "Teaching Culture in the Foreign Language Classroom," *Foreign Language Annals*, Vol. I, no. 2 (March 1968), pp. 204-217.

Bryan, Miriam M. "The MLA-Cooperative Foreign Language Tests: Tests with a New Look and a New Purpose," *DFL Bulletin*, Vol. VI, no. 2 (Dec. 1966) pp. 6-8.

Buiten, Roger and Harlan Lane. "A Self-Instructional Device for Conditioning Accurate Prosody," *International Review of Applied Linguistics*, Vol. III, no. 3 (1965), pp. 205-219.

Buros, Oscar K. (ed.). *The Sixth Mental Measurements Yearbook* (Highland Park, N. J.: Gryphon Press, 1965).

Carroll, John B. *The Foreign Language Attainments of Language Majors in the Senior Year: A Survey Conducted in U.S. Colleges and Universities.* (Cambridge, Mass.: Harvard University Graduate School of Education, 1967).

———. "The Prediction of Success in Intensive Foreign Language Training," in Glaser, Robert (ed.), *Training Research and Education* (New York: Rand McNally, 1962), pp. 1060-1100.

———. "The Psychology of Language Testing," in Davies, Alan (ed.), *Language Testing Symposium* (London: Oxford University Press, 1968), pp. 46–69.

———. "What Does The Pennsylvania Foreign Language Research Project Tell Us?," *Foreign Language Annals,* Vol. III, no. 2 (Dec. 1969), pp. 214-236.

Cartier, Francis A. "Criterion-Referenced Testing of Language Skills," *TESOL Quarterly,* Vol. II (1968), pp. 27-32.

Clark, John L. D. *Empirical Studies Related to the Teaching of French Pronunciation to American Students* (Cambridge, Mass.: Harvard University Graduate School of Education, 1967).

———. "MLA-Cooperative Foreign Language Tests," *Journal of Educational Measurement,* Vol. II, no. 2 (Dec. 1965), pp. 234-244.

———. "The Graduate School Foreign Language Requirement: A Survey of Testing Practices and Related Topics," *Foreign Language Annals,* Vol. II, no. 2 (Dec. 1968), pp. 150-164.

Cloos, Robert I. "A Four-Year Study of Foreign Language Aptitude at the High School Level," *Foreign Language Annals,* Vol. IV, no. 4 (May 1971), pp. 411-419.

Cooper, Robert L. "What Do We Learn When We Learn a Language?," *TESOL Quarterly,* Vol. IV, no. 4 (Dec. 1970), pp. 303-314.

Delattre, Pierre. "Testing Students' Progress in the Language Laboratory," *International Journal of American Linguistics* (Oct. 1960), pp. 77-92.

Diederich, Paul B. *Short-cut Statistics for Teacher-made Tests* (Princeton, N.J.: Educational Testing Service, 1964) (Evaluation and Advisory Series).

Dyer, Henry S. "Testing by Ear," *College Board Review* (May 1954), pp. 11-14.

Guerra, Emilio L., Abramson, David A. and Maxim Newmark. "The New York City Foreign Language Oral Ability Rating Scale," *Modern Language Journal,* Vol. XLVIII, no. 8 (Dec. 1964), pp. 486-489.

Hakstian, A. Ralph, *et al.* "The Pimsleur Modern Foreign Language Proficiency Tests," *Journal of Educational Measurement,* Vol. VI, no. 1 (1969), pp. 44-50.

Hall, Edward T. *The Silent Language* (New York: Doubleday, 1959).

Harris, David P. *Testing English as a Second Language* (New York: McGraw-Hill, 1969).

Hascall, Edward O. "Predicting Success in High School Foreign Language Study," *Personnel and Guidance Journal,* Vol. XL (Dec. 1961), pp. 361-367.

Jennings, Lee B. "Classroom Translation: A Lesser Bugbear?," *German Quarterly,* Vol. XL (Sept. 1967), pp. 518-529.

Lado, Robert. *Language Testing* (London: Longmans, Green, 1961). [Reprinted by McGraw-Hill, New York, 1964].

———. *Linguistics Across Cultures* (Ann Arbor: University of Michigan Press, 1957).

Lohnes, Walter F. W. "Teaching the Foreign Literature," in Birkmaier, Emma M. (ed.), *Britannica Review of Foreign Language Educa-*

tion, Vol. I (Chicago: Encyclopaedia Britannica, 1968), pp. 83-103.

Lutz, Marjorie. *The Development of Foreign Language Aptitude Tests: A Review of the Literature.* Test Development Report TDR-66-4 (Princeton, N.J.: Educational Testing Service, 1967).

Moulton, William G. *The Sounds of English and German* (Chicago: The University of Chicago Press, 1962).

Nostrand, Howard L. "Describing and Teaching the Sociocultural Context of a Foreign Language and Literature," in Valdman, Albert (ed.), *Trends in Language Teaching* (New York: McGraw-Hill, 1966), pp. 1-25.

Nostrand, Howard L. and Frances B. Nostrand. "Testing Understanding of the Foreign Culture," in Seelye, H. Ned (ed.), *Perspectives for Teachers of Latin American Culture* (Springfield, Illinois: Superintendent of Public Instruction, 1970), pp. 161-170.

O'Rourke, Everett V. "Evaluation and Testing," in Levenson, Stanley and William Kendrick (eds.), *Readings in Foreign Languages for the Elementary School* (Waltham, Mass.: Blaisdell, 1967), pp. 412-425.

Pickett, G. D. "A Comparison of Translation and Blank-filling as Testing Techniques," *English Language Teaching*, Vol. 23 (1968), pp. 21-26.

Pimsleur, Paul. "A French Speaking Proficiency Test," *French Review*, Vol. XXXIV (1961), pp. 470-479.

―――. "Testing Foreign Language Learning," in Valdman, Albert (ed.), *Trends in Language Teaching* (New York: McGraw-Hill, 1966), pp. 175-214.

Pimsleur, Paul, Donald M. Sundland, and Ruth D. McIntyre, "Under-Achievement in Foreign Language Learning," *International Review of Applied Linguistics*, Vol. II, no. 2 (1964), pp. 113-150.

Politzer, Robert L. *Foreign Language Learning: A Linguistic Introduction* (Englewood Cliffs, N. J.: Prentice-Hall, 1965).

Pulliam, Robert. *Application of the SCOPE Speech Interpreter in Experimental Educational Programs* (Fairfax, Va.: Pulliam and Associates, 1969).

―――. *Automatic Speech Recognition in the Teaching of Second Languages: An Annotated Bibliography* (Fairfax, Va.: Pulliam and Associates, 1970).

Remer, Ilo. *A Handbook for Guiding Students in Modern Foreign Languages* (Washington, D.C.: U.S. Government Printing Office, 1963).

Rivers, Wilga. "Listening Comprehension," in Donoghue, Mildred R. (ed.), *Foreign Languages and the Schools: A Book of Readings* (Dubuque, Iowa: Wm. C. Brown Company, 1967), pp. 189-200.

Rude, Ben D. "A Technique for Language Laboratory Testing," *Language Learning*, Vol. XVII (1967), pp. 151-153.

Savard, Jean-Guy. *Bibliographie analytique de tests de langue* (Quebec: Les Presses de l'Université Laval, 1969).

Scheider, Rose M. "Evolution of the Listening Comprehension Tests," *College Board Review* (Fall 1962), pp. 24-28.

Seelye, H. Ned. "Analysis and Teaching of the Cross-Cultural Context," in Birkmaier, Emma M. (ed.), *Britannica Review of Foreign Language Education*, Vol. I (Chicago: Encyclopaedia Britannica, 1968), pp. 37-81.

—————. "An Objective Measure of Biculturation: Americans in Guatemala, A Case Study," *Modern Language Journal*, Vol. LIII, No. 7 (Nov. 1969), pp. 503-514.

—————. "Field Notes on Cross-Cultural Testing," *Language Learning*, Vol. XVI, nos. 1-2 (1966), pp. 77-85.

—————. "Performance Objectives for Teaching Cultural Concepts," *Foreign Language Annals*, Vol. III, no. 1 (May 1970), pp. 566-578.

Seibert, Louise C. and Lester G. Crocker. *Skills and Techniques for Reading French* (New York: Harper and Row, 1958).

Spolsky, Bernard. "Language Testing: The Problem of Validation," *TESOL Quarterly*, Vol. II (June 1968), pp. 88-94.

Spolsky, Bernard, *et al.* "Preliminary Studies in the Development of Techniques for Testing Overall Second Language Proficiency," *Language Learning*, Special Issue No. 3 (Aug. 1968), pp. 79-98.

Stack, Edward M. *The Language Laboratory and Modern Language Teaching*, revised edition (New York: Oxford University Press, 1966).

Starr, Wilmarth H. "MLA Foreign Language Proficiency Tests for Teachers and Advanced Students," *PMLA*, Vol. LXXVII, no. 4, part 2 (1962), pp. 1-12.

Stockwell, Robert P. and J. Donald Bowen. *The Sounds of English and Spanish* (Chicago: The University of Chicago Press, 1965).

Upshur, John A. "Language Proficiency Testing and the Contrastive Analysis Dilemma," *Language Learning*, Vol. XII, no. 2 (1962), pp. 123-127.

Valette, Rebecca M. *Modern Language Testing: A Handbook* (New York: Harcourt, Brace, 1967).

—————. "The Pennsylvania Study, Its Conclusions and Its Implications," *Modern Language Journal*, Vol. LIII, no. 6 (Oct. 1969), pp. 396-404.

Von Wittich, Barbara. "Prediction of Success in Foreign Language Study," *Modern Language Journal*, Vol. XLVI, no. 5 (May 1962) pp. 208-212.

Woodford, Protase E. "Testing Procedures," in Walsh, Donald D. (ed.), *A Handbook for Teachers of Spanish and Portuguese* (Lexington, Mass.: D. C. Heath, 1969), pp. 89-107.

Index

Achievement testing, 3, 25–117
  See also Diagnostic achievement testing; General achievement testing
Advanced Placement Tests, 140, 146, 154, 155
Alternate forms
  of items, 36, 54
  of tests, 21, 154
Aptitude tests. *See* Foreign-language aptitude tests
Aural discrimination tests, 43–46

Biserial correlation, 160–161

Chance-success factor
  in free-response items, 54, 86
  in multiple-choice items, 34–37, 45, 47, 70
Character-formation tests, 106–107
Character-recognition tests, 94–96
Classroom observation, in speaking testing, 75
College Board Achievement Tests, 22, 153, 154–155
College Board Advanced Placement Tests, 155
College Entrance Examination Board, 153
College Placement Tests, 22
Common Concepts Foreign Language Tests, 158
Communicative proficiency
  definition, 119
  direct tests of, 121–130
  indirect measurement of, 130–132
  relationship to linguistic ability, 118–120
Contrastive analysis, 65–66
  of cultural patterns, 137
Cooperative Tests and Services, 157, 164
Copying tests. *See* Character-formation tests
Correlation
  definition, 12

role in indirect proficiency testing, 130–132
  role in prognostic testing, 13
Course grades
  in non-language subjects, 19–20
  in prior foreign-language courses, 20–21
Criterion measures, 12, 14
Culture testing, 134–140
  as explanation of cultural phenomena, 139–140
  as knowledge of civilization and fine arts, 134–136
  as knowledge of cultural patterns, 138–139
  as performance in host country situations, 138
Cutoff point, 23, 24

Diagnostic accuracy, factors affecting, 34–38
Diagnostic achievement testing, 3–4, 25–26, 34–38
Differential prediction, 18–19
Difficulty index, for test items, 160
Discrete items, 67–68
Distracter options, 65

Educational Testing Service, 39, 40, 61, 125, 127, 153, 154, 157, 164
English, use of in testing, 38–39, 47–48, 96–97
Expectancy tables, 23, 131–132

Fatigue, as factor in writing tests, 114
Foreign Language Aptitude Test (Revised), 15
Foreign-language aptititude tests, 2, 15–19, 22
  differential prediction using, 18
Foreign-language test modalities, 26–29
  factors in selection of, 29–42

171

Foreign Service Institute Absolute
Proficiency Rating, 121–125,
126, 128–129, 130
Frozen sentences, 112
FSI Interview. *See* Foreign Service
Institute
Absolute Proficiency Rating

General achievement testing, 4–5
definition, 25–26
of listening comprehension,
58–72
of reading, 103–106
of speaking, 86–94
of writing, 113–117
Graduate Record Examinations, 155
Graduate Record Examinations
Board, 153
Graduate School Foreign Language
Tests, 155

Halo effect, 117
Hybrid items, 107

Imitation, as speaking test proce-
dure, 79
Inter-rater reliability, 127
Intra-rater reliability, 127
Item analysis, 160–161
Item reliability. *See* Biserial corre-
lation
Item-writing techniques, multiple
choice, 62–67

Knowledge testing, 6, 133–147
See also Culture testing; Literature testing

Language Aptitude Battery. *See*
Pimsleur Language Aptitude
Battery
Language as a subject matter, 6
Language laboratory
informal monitoring in, 74–75
speaking test administration in,
73
Lexicon and morphology tests, 107–
113
Linguistic ability, relationship to
communicative proficiency,
118–120

Linguistic ambiguity, in multiple-
choice items, 37–38, 45, 50–
51, 99
Listening comprehension tests, 42–
72
See also Aural discrimination
tests; General achievement
tests; Listening grammar tests;
Listening vocabulary tests
Listening grammar tests, 53–58
Listening vocabulary tests, 46–53
Literary information testing, 142–
144
Literary interpretation testing, 144–
147
Literature testing, 140–147
See also Literary information
testing; Literary interpretation testing; Reading in literature course

Measure, 12
See also Predictor measures; Criterion measures
Memory load, 49, 59, 63, 89–90,
103–104
MLA-Cooperative Foreign Language Tests, 22, 33, 41, 131,
157, 159, 162, 163, 164
MLA Foreign Language Proficiency
Tests for Teachers and Advanced Students, 33, 130, 157,
159, 164, 165
Modalities. *See* Foreign-language
test modalities
Modern Language Aptitude Test,
15–16
comparison with other language-
aptitude tests, 17–19
Modern Language Aptitude Test—
Elementary, 16
comparison with other aptitude
tests, 17–19
Motivation, student, 31

National Teacher Examinations,
153, 156
Nonsense words, 53–54
Norm-referenced tests, 148–149
Norms and norming, 161–164

Odd-adjective problem, 105–106

Orthographic influence, in pronunciation testing, 80

Outside knowledge, 62–63

Passage length and number of test questions, 64, 67–68

Passages, selection of

  for listening comprehension tests, 60–62

  for reading comprehension tests, 103

  See also Topics, selection of

Peace Corps, 39, 61, 125, 131

Percentile bands, 162

Percentile ranks, 162

Pictorial materials, considerations in use of, 52

Pimsleur Language Aptitude Battery, 16–17

  comparison with other aptitude tests, 17–19

Pimsleur Modern Foreign Language Proficiency Tests, 22, 33, 131, 158, 163

Placement, 2, 10–24

  definition, 11–12

  of beginning students, 14–20

  of continuing students, 20–22

  operation of placement programs, 22–24

Predictor measures, 13, 14–22

  course grades, 19–20

  locally-constructed tests, 21–22

  prior language achievement measures, 20–21

  published tests, 22

Pretesting, 159–160

Proficiency testing, 5–6, 61–62, 118–132

  See also Communicative proficiency

Prognostic testing, 2, 9–24

  need for, 9–10

  See also Placement

Pronunciation tests, phonemic-level, 76–78

Pronunciation tests, phonetic-level, 78–81

Published tests, 148–165

  See also Locally-prepared tests; Standardized tests; Textbook-related tests

Rating scales. *See* Scoring scales

Reading grammar tests, 100–103

Reading in the literature course, 141–142

Reading tests, 94–106

  See also Character-recognition tests; General achievement testing; Reading grammar tests; Reading vocabulary tests

Reading vocabulary tests, 96–100

Response. *See* Foreign-language test modalities

Scaled scores, 154

Scholastic Aptitude Tests, 154

Score equating, 154

Scoring

  difficulty of scoring taped speaking tests, 73

  ease and reliability considerations, 39–42

  interpretation of general achievement test scores, 69–72

  mechanical scoring of speaking and writing tests, 40–41

  multiple-choice, 40

  of communicative proficiency tests, 126–129

  of general achievement speaking tests, 91–94

  of general achievement writing tests, 117

  of literary interpretation tests, 146–147

  See also Scoring scales

Scoring reliability

  of communicative proficiency tests, 126–129

  of fill-in writing test items, 111–112

  of free-response tests, 41–42

  of informal speaking tests, 75

  of multiple-choice tests, 40

Scoring scales
　and scoring reliability, 41
　for FSI interview, 122–123
　for general achievement speak-
　　ing tests, 92–93
　for informal speaking tests, 74–
　　75
　for literary interpretation tests,
　　147
　for phonetic-level pronunciation
　　tests, 78–79
　for writing tests, 112, 113, 117
Selection, 2, 10–11
Skills, separation of in testing, 32–
　34
Speaking grammar tests, 84–86
Speaking tests, 72–94
　alternatives to formal speaking
　　tests, 74–75
　indirect speaking tests, 30–31
　practical difficulties, 72–74
　See also General achievement
　　testing; Pronunciation tests,
　　phonemic-level; Pronunciation
　　tests, phonetic-level; Speak-
　　ing grammar tests; Speaking
　　vocabulary tests
Speaking vocabulary tests, 81–83
Spelling tests. *See* Lexicon and
　morphology tests
Standard error of test scores, 70–71
Standardized tests
　comparison to textbook-related
　　tests, 151–153
　definition, 148–149
　development procedures for,
　　158–161
　generally-available tests, 156–158
　measurement uses of, 164–165
　norming of, 161–164
　secure tests, 153–156

Stimulus. *See* Foreign language test
　modalities
Sub-scores, 5, 19, 93–94

Test development procedures, for
　standardized tests, 158–161
Test directions, for speaking and
　writing topics, 115
Test-wiseness, 69
Textbook-related tests, 149–153
　comparison to locally-developed
　　tests, 150–151
　comparison to standardized tests,
　　151–153
　definition, 148
Topics, selection of
　for literary interpretation tests,
　　145–146
　for "monologue" speaking tests,
　　87–88
　for writing tests, 114–115, 116–
　　117
　See also Passages, selection of
Trial period, in placement program,
　24

Validity study, 13, 22–23
Vocabulary tests, *See* Listening
　vocabulary tests; Reading vo-
　cabulary tests; Speaking vo-
　cabulary tests; Writing vocab-
　ulary tests

Work-sample tests. *See* Communi-
　cative proficiency
Writing tests, 106–117
　indirect writing tests, 31
　See also Character-formation
　　tests; General achievement
　　testing; Lexicon and morphol-
　　ogy tests